Stupid
Science

Other Books by Leland Gregory

Stupid Science

Weird Experiments, Mad Scientists, and Idiots in the Lab

Leland Gregory

3 1336 08447 3280

Andrews McMeel
Publishing, LLC
Kansas City • Sydney • London

ISBN-13: 978-0-7407-7990-9
ISBN-10: 0-7407-7990-7

Library of Congress Control Number: 2009925646

09 10 11 12 13 RR2 10 9 8 7 6 5 4 3 2 1

Book design by Holly Camerlinck
Illustrations by Robert Mag

www.andrewsmcmeel.com

Attention: Schools and Businesses

Andrews McMeel books are available at quantity discounts with bulk purchase for educational, business, or sales promotional use. For information, please write to: Special Sales Department, Andrews McMeel Publishing, LLC, 1130 Walnut Street, Kansas City, Missouri 64106.

Wide-Eyed Wonder

According to an article in the July 7, 2008, edition of the London newspaper *Daily Mail*, Britain's Sea Life Centre announced a study to determine whether octopuses use certain tentacles or random tentacles when faced with a complex situation. In order to test their hypothesis, the center announced they would give the octopuses Rubik's Cubes to play with.

"Larger Kangaroos
Leap Farther,
Researchers Find"

Los Angeles Times headline, November 2, 1995

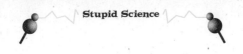
A Lack of Brains

Scientists at the Institute for Animal Health in Edinburgh secured a £217,000 government grant and spent five years trying to discover whether bovine spongiform encephalopathy (commonly called mad cow disease) had crossed the species barrier from cows to sheep. It came to light in October 2001 that the program was under investigation after it was discovered that scientists had inadvertently been testing cattle brains instead of sheep brains for the entire five years.

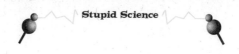

When Pigs Fly

Faced with the threat of the deadly swine flu, the U.S. government spent $135 million in 1976 on a national vaccination program. The vaccine was directly responsible for the deaths of twenty-three people, and hundreds more suffered reactions ranging from paralysis to heart attacks.

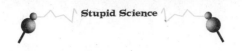

Just Monkeying Around

It's the age-old conundrum: Could an infinite number of monkeys with an infinite number of typewriters writing for an infinite amount of time reproduce the works of Shakespeare? Researchers at Plymouth University in England, not having an infinite amount of grant money, wanted to see what six Sulawesi crested macaque monkeys would write over a four-week period with a computer. According to a report in the May 9, 2003, issue of the *Guardian* of London, the simian Shakespeares composed roughly five pages of text between them, consisting mostly of the letter *S*. According to Professor Geoff Cox, who designed the test, the monkeys spent a lot of time sitting on the keyboard. "Another thing they were interested in was defecating and urinating all over the keyboard," added researcher Mike Phillips.

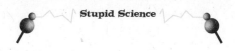
Don't Be So Testy!

Georgia State University psychology professor James Dabbs discovered in 1998 that trial lawyers (both male and female) have about 30 percent more testosterone in their bodies than other people. Dabbs stated in his article in the *Journal of Applied Social Psychology* that high testosterone levels are often linked to aggressiveness and antisocial behavior. We all knew that lawyers were full of something; now we know it's testosterone.

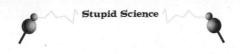

But with a Whimper

A science experiment at Winona High School in Texas turned out to be a real blast. With the approval of his physics teacher, a seventeen-year-old student brought in a homemade cannon designed to use gunpowder that "shoots a little projectile in the air," said school superintendent Rodney Fausett. But when the metal tube was being loaded with the gunpowder, it exploded, sending the "small little tube . . . through the wall of the building—a metal wall—so it had a pretty good oomph to it," said an investigator from the U.S. Bureau of Alcohol, Tobacco, Firearms and Explosives. According to a May 19, 2006, article in the *Dallas Morning News*, parents had expressed concern over the demonstration, but school officials blew them off.

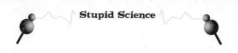

Primate of the Month

An article in the September 22, 2008, edition of *New Scientist* revealed that scientists at Emory University's primate research center in Atlanta, Georgia, conducted experiments to see whether chimps could remember other chimps through whole body integration (the ability to identify a whole object by seeing only a small portion of that body). Researchers concluded that chimps do have that ability because they identified, above mere random chance, other chimps in the program after being shown pictures of their butts.

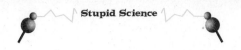

Size Does Matter

Research conducted by Indiana University on the differences between Australian dung beetles and U.S. dung beetles was published in the September 6, 2008, edition of *New Scientist*. The short and long of the results were this: Australian dung beetles have smaller horns and bigger penises, and the Americans are just the opposite. Researchers noted that in order to mate with females, American male dung beetles routinely fight other males, whereas the well-endowed Australian dung beetle relies more on trickery.

The Illinois Department
of Conservation spent
$180,000
to study the contents
of owl vomit.

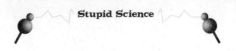
Calling Dr. Scholl

What do stinky cheese and unclean feet have in common?
They both attract mosquitoes. Scientists from all corners of
the globe gathered in Africa with wheels of smelly cheese in
an attempt to isolate the chemical that is common to both
cheese and stinky feet in hopes of using it as bait in mosquito
traps. According to a November 8, 1996, article from Reuters,
the scientific theory is based on research that hungry female
mosquitoes are attracted to such smells.

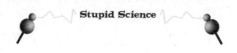

Green with Envy

Amateur scientists and hobbyists, who sometimes call themselves biohackers, are constantly at work in their garages or homemade laboratories making more than stink bombs. According to a January 1, 2009, article from the Associated Press, one amateur paid about $100 for jellyfish DNA, which contains a green fluorescent protein, and then spent $25 to build a DNA analyzer. She used the jellyfish DNA to alter yogurt bacteria so that when they detected melamine (a toxic chemical responsible for the 2008 Chinese milk scandal), they would glow green.

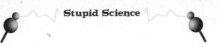

What's in a Name?

The Associated Press reported on March 29, 1998, about a study conducted by the University of California at San Diego that gave a lot of people an initial concern. The research disclosed that people whose initials spell out positive words live longer than those whose initials spell out negative words. "It's a little tiny depressant to be called PIG, or a little tiny boost to your esteem to be called ACE or WOW," says psychologist Nicholas Christenfeld, who along with two others called their hypothesis the theory of deadly initials. People whose initials spelled out words such as *VIP* or *GOD* lived an average of 4.48 years longer than the control group, whose initials had no distinctive qualities. The people with initials such as *DIE* or *BUM* died 2.8 years sooner than the control group.

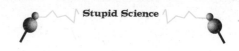

What's Got Your Goat?

As reported in a June 18, 2000, Associated Press article, Nexia Biotechnologies, located outside Plattsburgh, New York, successfully bred 150 goats with a gene from a spider to produce "BioSteel." The company has since been researching ways to use the goat milk with recombinant silk proteins to produce an extraordinarily strong and lightweight silk fiber for use in aerospace and medical applications and in bulletproof clothing.

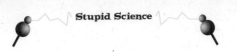

Ant-Agonize

According to Frankfurt University researchers, ants living in bamboo stems in Malaysian rain forests are real pissers. Their research, as reported in the January 6, 2001, issue of *New Scientist*, revealed that in order to keep their nests dry the ants drink the water that leaks in, then they go outside and urinate. They continue the process until their nest is dry, giving new meaning to the word *pissant*.

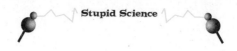

I Don't Give a Crap!

Chagas's disease, which kills fifty thousand people a year in Central and South America, is spread by bites of the kissing bug (triatomine), which infects a human after biting into the skin for nutrition. But it isn't the bite that causes the infection; it's the fact that the bug eats its parents' dung, which contains a parasitic protozoan. Charles Beard told the *Los Angeles Times* in an article from April 9, 2001, that he has created genetically modified dung that looks, smells, and, according to the kissing bugs, tastes just like the poop their mom made. The faux feces is made from ammonia, ink, and guar gum and contains special bacteria that prevent the disease from spreading.

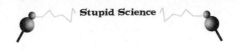

Trout Teaser

Scientists from Sweden's National Board of Fisheries reported in a March 15, 2001, issue of *New Scientist* that after observing 117 pairs of trout engaged in sex, they discovered that nearly 50 percent of the time the female trout "faked it." Trout reproduce by means of a courtship dance that ends with the male and female simultaneously releasing their sperm and eggs. But the researchers noticed that in half the cases, at the climax of the dance, the male released his sperm, but the female withheld her eggs. It is hypothesized that the female intentionally does this to preserve her eggs in case she meets up with a more desirable male.

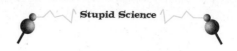

Cat Calls

Victor Marchetti, a former Central Intelligence Agency officer, told London's *Daily Telegraph* in an article from November 4, 2001, about a secret surveillance project in the 1960s code named "Acoustic Kitty." Marchetti explained that a cat was surgically implanted with batteries and wires and had an antenna threaded through its tail in order to eavesdrop on enemies and transmit their conversations back to a receiving station. The project was developed over a period of five years, but before the first high-frequency feline could be tuned in, it was run over and killed by a taxi.

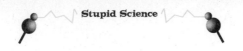

Pig in a Poke

Some people will go to any lengths to get kids to eat vegetables. Reuters reported on January 24, 2002, that researchers at Kinki University in Nara, Japan, had successfully spliced spinach genes into pig DNA, making it the first ever mammal–plant combination. Professor Akira Iritani stated that the harvested meat would be "more healthy" than normal pork, but, he added, "the significance of this success is more academic than practical." However, if Professor Iritani had also combined spinach with a chicken, we could have green eggs and ham.

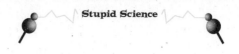

The Booger Man

Scientists have discovered that even though eating your own boogers isn't socially acceptable, it isn't dangerous, either. An article in the December 20, 2001, issue of Toronto's *National Post* reported that a group of scientists have dedicated their lives to the study of mucus in spite of the social stigma associated with expelled secretions (usually the stuff kids laugh about). They claimed that the underresearched mucus can hold a wealth of scientific knowledge and cited as evidence a certain mucin (a protein contained in mucus) that seems to block the body's ability to fight a cancer cell; they hypothesized that eliminating that mucin could eliminate the cancer. If you think mucus research is funny, it's snot.

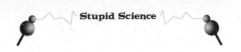

Hop to It

It is widely understood that methane gas is a prime contributor to ozone depletion and the dreaded global warming, and an enormous amount of methane is expelled through cattle and sheep flatulence (*fartis maximus*). As reported in a May 3, 2002, Associated Press article, scientists at the Department of Primary Industries in Queensland, Australia, will test forty potentially methane-reducing bacteria found in the digestive tracts of kangaroos because, for reasons yet unknown, kangaroos are less flatulent than other animals.

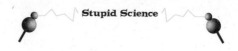

The Eyes Have It

Spanish biologist J. J. Negro of the Estación Biológica de Doñana (Biological Station of Doñana) in southwestern Spain reported in the journal *Nature* in April 2002 that female Egyptian vultures are attracted to males whose faces are the brightest yellow. In order to increase the yellow hue in their faces, the males must gorge themselves on excrement. Carotenoids, natural fat-soluble pigments found principally in plants and algae and abundant in dung, enhance the yellow color around the male vultures' eyes. But it's not just that the female finds the color more attractive; the brightest-colored male vulture is also the strongest because only strong vultures can survive eating the bacteria-laden feces.

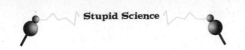

Greater Love Hath No Spud Than This

Scientists at the Max Planck Institute for Plant Breeding Research in Cologne, Germany, have genetically engineered a potato with suicidal tendencies. The self-sacrificing spud was designed to meet its maker if attacked by potato blight fungi. According to a May 20, 1996, report in the *Chicago Sun-Times*, it thus saves its fellow potatoes from the same fate.

The *New England Journal of Medicine*
reported on September 19, 2002,
that children have a much lower rate
of asthma if they have been exposed
to dirt and dust growing up.

In 1991, after construction of the
17-ton Compton Gamma-Ray Observatory
satellite went $40 million over budget,
NASA sent a $5 million bonus check
to the contractor.

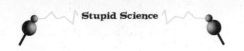

Klaatu Barada Nikto

A June 20, 2002, article in the *Age* (Melbourne) reported that Gaak, a robot programmed to equip other robots to think for themselves, escaped from a holding pen at the Magna Science Adventure Centre in Rotherham, England. Gaak was being held for repairs when he escaped and made it as far as the parking lot before bumping into a visitor's car. Said Professor Noel Sharkey, "[The robots] have all learned a significant amount and are becoming more intelligent by the day."

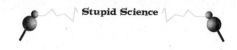

You Do Have to Be a Rocket Scientist

On August 8, 2001, the NASA spacecraft *Genesis* was launched with its intended mission to sample particles from the solar wind, which it did successfully. As it was entering Earth's atmosphere on September 8, 2004, however, the landing parachute failed to open, and the capsule smashed into the ground at high speed. An investigation was conducted into the faulty parachute, and it was discovered that the internal mechanisms of the acceleration sensor had been installed backward.

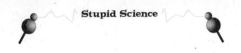

The Thing with Two Heads

New Scientist magazine reported on December 3, 2002, that researchers from the Jichi Medical University in Tochigi, Japan, had surgically removed the heads of infant rats and, after holding onto them for ninety minutes, grafted them onto the thighs of adult rats. For the next three weeks the brains of the infant rats continued to develop, and their mouths began opening and closing as if expecting milk. The researchers were quoted as saying they believed their experiments to be an "excellent model" for brain development in human babies. And the thing from which nightmares are made.

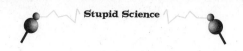

It's Good to Be the King

Australian biologist Mark Elgar wrote an article in the July 23, 2003, issue of *Nature* magazine praising the lifestyle of the tiny male Zeus bug. The little bug enjoys a work-free existence because the female provides for all his needs; she piggy-backs him from destination to destination, supplies all his food, and gives him as much sex as he desires. It's no mystery why the insect is named after Zeus, the Greek king of the gods, but the mystery, according to Elgar, is how the male Zeus got to be so lucky.

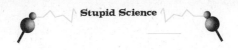

A Killer Whale

People think flatulence is gross or funny, but scientists from
the Australian Antarctic Division think it's awesome. As part
of their research mission to track the habits of whales, the
team was busy tagging the enormous mammals with satellite
tracking devices when something never captured before
occurred: a whale farted. According to a September 14, 2003,
article in the *Australian*, the team believes they have the first-
ever photo of the water pattern made by a whale passing
wind. And according to researchers, they got more than just
an eyeful; they got a noseful, too. "We got away from the bow
of the ship very quickly," said Nick Gales. "It does stink."

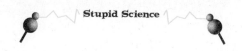
If Life Gives You Lemons

Carl Hanson of St. Paul, Minnesota, filed for and received U.S. patent no. 6,457,474 in 2002 for a breakthrough in the treatment of heart-related chest pain. According to an August 2003 article in *Scientific American*, Hanson's newly patented invention for angina pain is to drink limeade from concentrate. His accepted patent application explains that the remedy worked for him and then goes into detail about how the newly patented invention works: Buy cans of concentrated limeade, follow the instructions on the can, and drink it (the patent also covers limeade taken intravenously).

ALL IN A DAY'S WORK

Each year *Popular Science* magazine lists the worst jobs in science. Here are some of the top fifteen from the October 2003 issue:

7. Researchers who analyze the contents of a cow's stomach by reaching into the cow's paunch to retrieve it.

----

4. Malaria researchers who endure three-hour shifts of being bitten up to fifteen times a minute by mosquitoes.

----

1. Being one of gastroenterologist Michael Levitt's "flatus odor judges," who sniff and rate for strength as many as a hundred tubes of flatulence hand collected from subjects who were fed pinto beans.

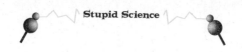

Upright Endorsements

Jeff Meldrum, a professor of anatomy and anthropology at Idaho State University in Pocatello, was quoted in an October 23, 2003, article in *National Geographic News* as saying, "Given the scientific evidence that I have examined, I'm convinced there's a creature out there that is yet to be identified." Not big news until you realize he's talking about Bigfoot (also known as Sasquatch, the Abominable Snowman, the Yeti, or the Yowie Man). And he's not alone. Noted chimpanzee researcher Jane Goodall also believes wholeheartedly in the existence of the creatures.

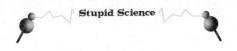
Nothing on the Ball

British scientist David Gems of London's University College, as reported in a May 24, 1997, article in *New Scientist*, provided evidence that males might live longer than females if not for their intense sex drive. He studied normal male marsupial mice, which "spend 5 to 11 hours a day copulating" and die after only a few weeks, and compared them with castrated marsupial mice, which can live for years. In terms of humans, Gems cited a 1969 study of 319 castrated men (eunuchs) who lived an average of 13.5 years longer than comparable men who still had their testicles. It might be true that castrated men live longer than normal men, but why would they want to?

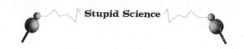
You're Pulling My Finger

Methane gas isn't responsible only for helping to destroy the ozone layer. It can also be deadly—as in "silent but deadly." Research conducted in 2000 at the University of Amsterdam, the Netherlands, confirmed that being in close quarters for a prolonged period of time with a flatulent family member, friend, or co-worker can weaken the immune system significantly and in some cases be fatal. Flatulent gas is "like second-hand smoke and is poisonous to the people that breathe it," explained Dr. Hans Sholten.

"Broads Give $100 Million to Research"

Los Angeles Daily News headline, June 19, 2003 (referring to money given by Eli and Edythe Broad, pronounced like *road*)

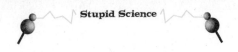

House of Buggin'

Two prominent Cornell University entomologists, Quentin Wheeler and Kelly B. Miller, paid homage to three prominent politicians by naming three new species of slime mold–eating beetles after them. The new beetles were named after president George W. Bush (*Agathidium bushi*), vice president Dick Cheney (*Agathidium cheneyi*), and secretary of defense Donald Rumsfeld (*Agathidium rumsfeldi*). Researchers explained in an April 14, 2005, Associated Press article that they "admire these leaders as fellow citizens" and swore they did it out of respect.

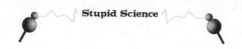

Here's a Little
Extra Something for You

Fiona Hunter, a researcher from England's Cambridge University, studied the mating habits of penguins for five years, and her results were summarized in a February 26, 1998, report on BBC News. Hunter discovered that some females allow males other than their mates to have intercourse with them in exchange for stones, with which they build their nests. She also noted that some males, as a form of performance pay raise, kick in a few more stones after they're finished. Hunter believes this is the first observance of prostitution in animals other than humans.

A winner of the

2008 Ig Nobel Prize

was a Japanese device called

the

"Bow-Lingual,"

which analyzes the tone of a dog's bark
and relays its mood.

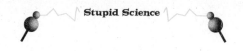

A Visit from Aunt Flo

During a conference in Brisbane, Australia, Dr. Thomas Perls, director of the New England Centenarian Study at Boston University Medical School, announced that his research has led him to believe that women live longer than men because they menstruate. According to an article in the March 19, 2005, issue of Australia's newspaper *News Limited*, Perls explained to the crowd that he routinely donates blood because iron loss through bleeding inhibits the growth of free radicals that age cells. "I menstruate," he said, "but only every eight weeks."

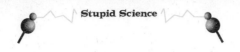

The Sacred Cow

According to a February 2005 article in the *Times* of London, animal welfare professors at Britain's Bristol University explained that they were prepared to present research findings to the June conference on Compassion in World Farming. They said their findings would show that cows experience emotions (fear and happiness), can form friendships, and are good at problem solving (brain waves measured with electro-encephalography showed peaks as a cow sought a path to food). They also discovered that cows can be moody and are capable of holding a grudge against another cow for months or even years.

Just My Luck

When buttered bread or toast falls off a table and lands butter side down, it is usually referred to as proof of one's bad luck. But Robert Matthews of Aston University in Birmingham, England, has postulated that "toast falling off the breakfast table lands butter side down because the universe is made that way." He says he proved it, using math (*European Journal of Physics*, 16: 172, 176, 1995). Actually, it has more to do with gravity and the distance from the table to the floor. Simply put, the falling toast doesn't have enough time to make a full rotation in order to land buttered side up.

Matthews proposed several ways to counter the "butter down" syndrome: Eat from tables 10 feet high, eat small squares of toast, tie the toast to a cat (which of course always lands on its feet), or, if you see the toast falling from the table, smack it to give it more rotations and improve your chances that it will land butter side up.

Animal House

According to a World Wildlife Fund report summarized in a
December 15, 2008, article in the *Times*, over the last decade
more than one thousand new animal species have been
discovered in the area surrounding the Mekong River (in
Cambodia, Laos, Thailand, and Vietnam). The newly discovered
species include striped rabbits, a spider larger than a hat,
and a pink millipede that produces cyanide.

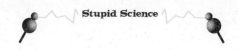

Bridal Suite at the Roach Motel

As reported in a July 24, 2001, article in *Scientific American*, scientists from Manchester, England, proposed at a conference that as a female cockroach's biological clock runs down, she lowers her standards for a mate.

$$g(z, \mu) = \int f(x) e^{-\mu x} \, dx$$

Support [

$$h(x, y) = \sum_{i=0}^{\infty} g(x) e^{-\mu x}$$

$$\frac{(\ln x - \mu)^2}{2\sigma^2}$$

$$x, \mu, \sigma$$

$$e^{\mu + \sigma^2/2}$$

"Psychologists Dissect the Multiple Meanings of Meow"

Headline from a May 30, 2003, article in the *Alameda Times-Star* about a study on how cats change the tone of their meow to garner human attention for various purposes

$$\int x f(x) \, dx$$

$$g(k) = \exp$$

$$e^{\mu - \sigma^2}, \quad (e^{\sigma^2} - 1) e^{2\mu + \sigma^2}$$

$$\text{Entropy} \quad \frac{1}{2} + \frac{1}{2}$$

This Is Only a (Science) Test
#1

The following are actual answers to questions on science exams.

Q: Name the four seasons.

A: Salt, pepper, mustard, and vinegar.

Q: Explain one of the processes by which water can be made safe to drink.

A: Flirtation makes water safe to drink because it removes large pollutants like grit, sand, dead sheep, and canoeists.

Q: How is dew formed?

A: The sun shines down on the leaves and makes them perspire.

Q: How can you delay milk turning sour?

A: Keep it in the cow.

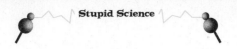

A Bug's Life

Naturalist John Lubbock conducted experiments on ants and alcohol in the late 1800s and noticed similarities between the insects and humans. He observed intoxicated ant behavior in 1888 and noted that drunken ants were carried home by their nest mates, but drunken strangers (not from the same nest) were pushed into a ditch.

Dude Looks Like a Lady

Mark Norman, an Australian biologist from James Cook University, reported in July 1999 that male cuttlefish (which belong to the same class as squid and octopuses) that are too small to attract a female have the ability to change shape and color to mimic a female. They are then able to mingle with male–female couples and, when the male is distracted, turn back into the masculine form and steal the female away.

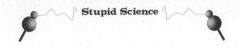

Break Like the Wind

In an August 3, 1995, article in the *Edmonton Journal*, respected British scientist Colin Leakey complained that his research has been woefully underfunded. Leakey is looking into the causes of flatulence.

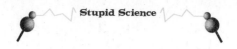

Making a Real Boob
out of Yourself

Kevin Cronin, a tissue engineer at the Bernard O'Brien Institute of Microsurgery in Melbourne, Australia, speaking at a meeting of the Royal Australasian College of Surgeons, reported that he has successfully grown breast and fat tissue in rats, mice, and rabbits. According to a May 23, 2001, article in *New Scientist*, Cronin claimed his findings could be used in the field of breast reconstruction after mastectomy, and "there is an obvious spin-off into breast augmentation and facial aesthetic surgery."

"British Ducks
Have Regional Accents,
Researchers Say"

BBC News headline, June 4, 2004

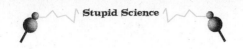

I'm So Lonesome I Could Die

James Gundlach, a sociologist at Auburn University in Alabama, noticed that the suicide rate in Nashville, Tennessee, was much higher than in forty-nine other large metropolitan areas. He and his students wanted to find out why. Steven Stack of Wayne State University in Detroit joined Gundlach's team, and they concluded that, according to an October 1, 2004, article in the *Guardian*, more people who listen to country music tend to kill themselves.

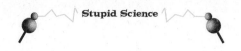
What's the Buzz About?

New Scientist magazine reported on September 9, 2004, about a team of British scientists who are developing a robot that will produce its own electric power by eating flies. The power system of the EcoBot II was created to break down the sugar in the flies' bodies by digesting them in specially designed fuel cells that convert the sugar into electrons. Although an energetically autonomous robot is a breakthrough, there is a drawback: In order to entice the flies needed to power the robot, it will have to be smeared with sewage or excrement.

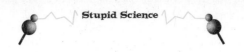
Good to the Last Drop

"People should not be apprehensive. When you eat meat, there is blood in that," said Dr. Ludmila Antipova, a scientist at Voronezh State Technological Academy in Russia. Dr. Antipova, head of the Department of Meat and Meat Products, and her research team have found a way to turn blood into chocolate-filled biscuits, yogurt, and drinks. As reported in an August 1, 2004, article in the *Telegraph* of London, Dr. Antipova said her team's blood-based foods are delicious and taste as good as the real thing. I guess you could order one from type A and one from type B.

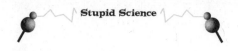

A Head of the Game

Airport security has tightened significantly since
September 11, 2001, and it's difficult to get anything through
screening—especially a severed head. A man who claimed
to be a biology professor, flying from Boston's Logan
International Airport to Denver, asserted that he found a dead
seal on Revere Beach and cut off its head for educational use.
The Associated Press reported on March 22, 2004, that the
man was permitted to board the aircraft, but the seal's head
was confiscated.

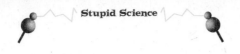

Better Living Through Chemicals

When city officials in Aliso Viejo, in Orange County, California, heard that Styrofoam containers were produced using the dangerous chemical "dihydrogen monoxide," they jumped into action. The concerned and socially responsible councilors proposed going before the city legislature to outlaw the potentially deadly substance from within the city boundaries, but they discovered something. The Associated Press reported in a March 15, 2004, article that embarrassed officials soon learned that dihydrogen monoxide, or H_2O for short, is the chemical formula for water. "It's embarrassing," said city manager David J. Norman. "We had a paralegal who did bad research."

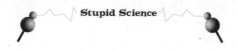

The Dilbert Factor

A research team in Sweden headed by Dr. Dagmar Andersson studied five hundred heart attack patients and discovered, to their amazement, that 62 percent didn't present with the common risk factors associated with heart disease. The researchers discovered that the patients had one thing in common: "Almost all of these low-risk patients told us they worked with people so stupid they can barely find their way from the parking lot to their office," Andersson said in an August 17, 2005, article in the *Toronto Star*. In a number of cases the heart attack came within twelve hours of dealing with an imbecile. The researchers' findings showed that working with stupid people can kill you.

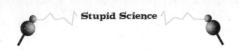

Bowled Away by Research

Researchers at the University of Arizona in Tucson reported in a June 13, 1998, article in *New Scientist* on the cleanest and dirtiest areas in an average home. Not surprisingly, their study found that kitchen cutting boards and used dishcloths had the highest bacteria counts, but what was shocking was the cleanest area. "What we found, and we are still theorizing as to why," said study leader Pat Rusin, "is that even before we introduced any disinfectant, the toilet seat was always the cleanest site."

"Flies Are Like Us: Scientists"

Australia's *News Limited* headline, July 8, 2003

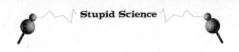

A Sticky Situation

Brian Gettelfinger and Edward Cussler turned up wearing snug-fitting swimming trunks to claim their 2004 Ig Nobel Prize in chemistry, reported *New Scientist* on January 10, 2005. The duo had finally solved a problem that even Sir Isaac Newton and Christian Huygens argued over. Is a person able to swim faster in water or in a syrupy mixture? Turns out that Newton's hypothesis was wrong. According to experiments conducted by Gettelfinger and Cussler, a person can swim equally fast in either liquid.

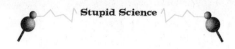

We're Number One!

In 2007, scientists at Procter & Gamble named the city of Phoenix, Arizona, the sweatiest city in the United States. Sweating an average of more than a quart an hour (equivalent to two and a half cans of your favorite soft drink), the citizens of Phoenix are preeminent in perspiration. Procter & Gamble researcher Dr. Tim Long, quoted in a June 18, 2007, PR Newswire article, ranked the top hundred sweaty cities, placing Phoenix at number one and San Francisco as the least sweaty city at number one hundred.

$$g(x,\mu) = \int_{-\infty}^{\infty} f(x) e^{-\mu x} \, dx$$

$$h(x,y) = \sum_{i=0}^{\infty} g_i(x) e^{-\mu x}$$

$$-\frac{(\ln x - \mu)}{2\sigma^2}$$

$$x, \mu, \sigma) = \frac{1}{} e$$

According to an October 21, 2002,
Reuters article, the North Korean
government gave its annual prize
in science to Pyongyang Hospital
for creating a rhubarb-and-marijuana
remedy that is "97 percent effective"
in curing constipation.

$$\int x \, f(x) \, dx \qquad g(k) = \exp$$

$$e^{\mu - \sigma^2}, \quad (e^{\sigma^2} - 1) e^{2\mu + \sigma^2}$$

Entropy $\frac{1}{2} + \frac{1}{2}$

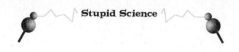

Striking Out in Science

According to a January 26, 2003, article in the *Guardian*, the U.S. Bureau of Land Management banned professional and amateur engineers of Utah's Salt Lake Astronomical Society from conducting a simulated meteor impact study on the salt flats. The scientific society was informed by the bureau that it was a dangerous and poorly thought-out idea to drop bowling balls from an airplane as part of their experiment because a lot of people worked in the area.

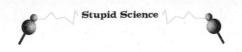

Frequent Flier

"Quite simply, they are going to be seasick until they have managed to acclimatize," said Johanna Bergstrom-Roos, a spokeswoman for the Esrange Space Center in Kiruna, Sweden, referring to a tank full of fish scheduled to be shot into space. For approximately six minutes, the tiny cichlid fish will experience weightlessness, and when they return to Earth, their inner ears will be examined. According to a February 21, 2008, report by the Swedish Space Corporation, scientists are testing a theory that the otolith, a structure in the inner ear, may determine sensitivity to motion sickness in both humans and fish.

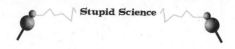

Not Nice to Mice

As reported in a July 29, 2007, article in the *Times*, researchers from Johns Hopkins University announced that they have successfully engineered the first mouse with a mental disorder. The schizophrenic mouse was created to help scientists understand the psychiatric disorder in humans. In an August 22, 2007, article in *Nature*, Duke Medical Center researchers announced similar success engineering mice with obsessive–compulsive disorder.

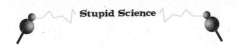

Cliché Come to Life

As reported in the journal *Lancet* and in a July 20, 2007, article in *New Scientist*, French neurologists using magnetic resonance imaging and computed tomography scanning on a normally functioning forty-four-year-old man discovered, to their surprise, that he had a brain "more than 50 percent to 75 percent" smaller than average. Lionel Feuillet, a neurologist at the Mediterranean University in Marseille, France, said the man's skull was filled mainly with fluid, leaving little more than a thin sheet of brain tissue. The unnamed man is a married father of two children and works as a civil servant in the French government.

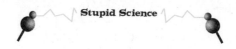

A Ray of Hope

Reuters reported in an article on June 25, 2007, that Arab researchers, writing in the *American Journal of Clinical Nutrition*, announced that Middle Eastern women who dress in traditional hijab or burka outfits that cover the head, face, and majority of the body have significant deficiencies in vitamin D because the essential vitamin is obtained primarily through exposure to sunlight.

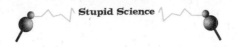

After a While, Crocodile

In order to get close enough to the enormous Nile crocodiles to attach data monitors to their tails, Dr. Brady Barr, a reptile specialist with the National Geographic TV channel, donned a crocodile suit and crawled to them. Barr, who also smeared hippopotamus dung on himself to mask his human scent, approached the twenty-foot-long reptiles in Tanzania and began tagging them as part of his research. The *Daily Mirror* of London described Barr's activities in a June 13, 2007, article and reported that the scariest moment involved not the crocodiles but a curious hippopotamus that was attracted by the smell of the dung.

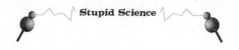
The Nose Knows

Human olfaction, or sense of smell, is greatly enhanced by mucus in the nose that captures odorant molecules and dissolves them so they can interact with receptors that produce signals our brain interprets as a smell. Not bad for snot, is it? According to a *New Scientist* article dated April 25, 2007, researchers from Warwick University in Coventry in the United Kingdom have developed an artificial mucus to use in their electronic noses. Electronic noses, or e-noses, are used commercially for quality control in food manufacturing and can detect diseases such as cancer. But e-noses are far less sensitive than biological ones because of the absence of mucus.

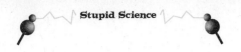

That Rings a Bell

One of the most famous experiments ever conducted was
that of Ivan Pavlov, who fed dogs while a bell was rung. After
a while, whenever the bell was rung, the dogs salivated
involuntarily, even without the presence of the food, an effect
known as a conditioned reflex. On June 13, 2007, Reuters
reported on a Tohoku University (Sendai, Japan) researcher
who found not only that cockroaches have memories and the
ability to learn but also that they can be taught, using a specific
odor, to salivate.

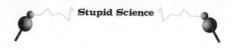

Comedy in Combat

The *San Antonio Express-News* reported on December 14, 2001, about a San Antonio research facility that developed a nonlethal military weapon dubbed "banana peel in a can." The substance is a super-slippery spray the Marine Corps envisions as useful to deter mobs that are advancing on military installations or embassies. According to the article, test subjects were unable to walk across a lawn treated with the slippery substance and were strapped into safety harnesses to prevent injury during their pratfalls.

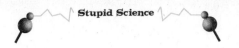

Two-Ply Scroll

The Essenes were a religious sect that was one of the three major divisions of the Jewish religion during the time of Christ. The Essenes disappeared after A.D. 70. They are remembered primarily as the authors of the Dead Sea Scrolls. Their disappearance was a mystery until a team of researchers stumbled on a likely cause: They were shy about their toilet habits. According to a November 15, 2006, report in London's *Independent*, researchers found evidence of abundant fecal bacteria in a secluded area. Because it was written in the scrolls that the Essenes didn't go to the bathroom in the open, the researchers deduced that because their excrement wasn't exposed to the sun's bacteria-killing effects, they could have died off as a result of infections.

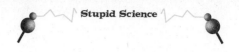

By Name and Nature

An article in the January 24, 2007, *Boston Globe* reported that biologists at Germany's University of Jena announced that after three years of research, they were canceling a long-term project on animal movements because they were tired of waiting for Mats, a sloth in the experiment, who refused to move from his perch. "We even tried feeding him pasta and boiled eggs," a despondent researcher reported.

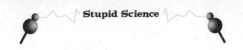

A Real Injury Lawyer

In their article "Potential Risk Factors for Prolonged Disability After Whiplash Injury: A Prospective Study" (Australian Broadcasting Corporation, April 12, 2001), a research team from South Australia's University of Adelaide, reporting on their preliminary findings, disclosed that some whiplash victims' pain and disability are prolonged more by "litigation" than by "damage to [the particular] joint."

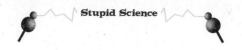

The Blue Flu

The University of Buffalo Research Institute on Addictions in New York issued a press release dated May 9, 2002, revealing the results of a $4-million study. They concluded that employees who drink heavily the night before are more likely to call in sick to work the next morning. Believe it or not!

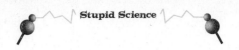

High-Pressure Situation

The *Mainichi Daily News*, the English-language version of Japan's Mainichi Newspapers, reported in an October 19, 2002, article about the results of a study on people who follow the rules for good health (e.g., healthful diet, no smoking, adequate sleep). The study, conducted at Tokyo's Jikei University, found that the blood pressure of people who followed the rules was about 6 percent higher than that of people who didn't care about their health.

"Nerds to Auction Themselves to Women"

Newsday headline, September 26, 2007

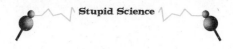

Stamp of Approval

The *Federation of American Scientists Secrecy News* reported on April 2, 2003, that the Central Intelligence Agency (CIA) had arranged an open panel meeting of top scientists in January to discuss potential use of biological warfare by terrorists. The panel concluded that although there were certain risks in making their findings public, openness was of the utmost importance. In April of that year, the CIA suppressed the panel's conclusion on openness as top secret and classified.

This Is Only a (Science) Test #2

The following are actual answers to questions on science exams.

Q: What causes the tides in the oceans?

A: The tides are a fight between the Earth and the Moon. All water tends to flow toward the Moon, because there is no water on the Moon, and nature hates vacuum. I forget where the sun joins in this fight.

Q: What are steroids?

A: Things for keeping carpets still on the stairs.

Q: What happens to your body as you age?

A: When you get old, so do your bowels and you get inter-continental.

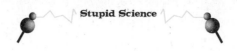

A Little Dab'll Do Ya

Ukrainian scientists told the Agence France-Presse news service in a story filed on April 28, 2003, that worms that survived the April 26, 1986, nuclear accident at the Chernobyl Nuclear Power Plant in the Soviet Union (where radioactivity is still many times higher than normal) are reproducing at a higher rate and are more sexually active than they were before the disaster.

Dan Ariely

won the

2008 Ig Nobel Prize

in

medicine

for demonstrating that expensive placebos
are more effective than inexpensive placebos.

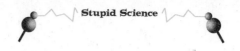

You Said a Mouthful

Receiving the Texas Academy of Science's Distinguished Texas Scientist award in March 2006, Eric Pianka, the Denton A. Cooley Centennial Professor of Integrative Biology and an expert on overpopulation, said, "The world will be much better off when only ten or twenty percent of us are left."

Over the average human lifetime, a person will produce 25,000 quarts of saliva, enough to fill two swimming pools.

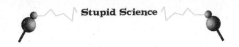

Two Heads Are Better Than One

A National Geographic TV special that ran in January 2007 focused on the Cold War struggle between U.S. and Soviet scientists and their rush to perform successful head transplants. One example was Russian Vladimir Demikhov's short-lived success in grafting a puppy's head and upper body onto the neck of a mastiff (the two apparently tolerated each other until the puppy died four days later). Then there was American Robert White of Cleveland, Ohio, who reportedly did a brain transplant on a dog and tracked which characteristics of the donor brain transferred to the new dog's body.

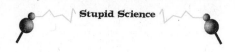

Cleaning Up Cancer

Writing in the December 2006 *Cancer Epidemiology Biomarkers & Prevention* report, German cancer researchers noted that any exercise is good for women because it helps ward off breast cancer in premenopausal women. But the report continued to say that housework (e.g., vacuuming, sweeping) works for all women (premenopausal and postmenopausal) and is superior to recreational physical activity.

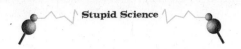
Domo Arigatō, Mr. Roboto

According to a paper solicited for the British government's chief scientific adviser and head of the Government Office for Science, Sir David King said, if advances in artificial intelligence (AI) continue to progress at their current rate, robots may eventually have to be given legal rights. One AI researcher said, "If [robots are] granted full rights, states will be obligated to provide full social benefits to them including income support, housing, and possibly robo-healthcare to fix the machines over time." The *Financial Times* of London reported in an article on December 19, 2006, that the study also proposed that robots might have to pay taxes and could be drafted into the armed forces.

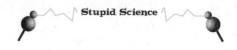

What's in the Soup?

A notorious former open pit copper mine, the Berkeley Pit in Butte, Montana, is filled with water 900 feet deep and laden with heavy metals and dangerous chemicals, including cadmium, zinc, arsenic, and sulfuric acid. It is considered to be the nation's largest environmental disaster site, and it is one of the government's largest Superfund projects. But according to an ABC News report from October 10, 2006, Montana Tech researchers, writing in the *Journal of Organic Chemistry*, have found more than 160 types of "extremophiles" (fungal and bacterial organisms that thrive in toxicity) in the pit and have demonstrated that some are effective against certain cancer cells such as lung and ovarian cancers.

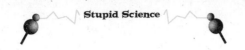

What's That Fowl Odor?

Working through a state-funded grant, researchers at Clemson University in South Carolina have been trying to make chicken poop smell better. According to an October 23, 1998, Associated Press article, professor Glenn Birrenkott reported that his team has made progress in their olfactory quest by adding garlic powder to the chickens' feed. It also makes their eggs taste better, said Birrenkott, and "it makes the poultry house smell like a pizzeria instead of manure."

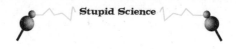

Writers Who Left

James Kaufman of the Learning Research Institute at California State University at San Bernardino studied authors and writers and came to the dramatic conclusion that "poets died significantly younger than both fiction writers and non-fiction writers." But the plot thickens: "Female poets were much more likely to suffer from mental illness than any other kind of writer and more likely than other eminent women," according to the November 10, 2003, issue of *The American Psychologist.* Kaufman took a dramatic pause and then remarked, "I've dubbed this the 'Sylvia Plath Effect.'"

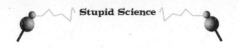

Crustacean Station

Biologist David Scholnick of Pacific University (Forest Grove, Oregon) doesn't go to many cocktail parties. He's more interested in what you dip in cocktail sauce: shrimp. Scholnick, who studies the effects of infections on shrimp and monitors their blood lactate levels, has created a tiny treadmill on which the shrimp run. "As far as I know," Scholnick told LiveScience.com on October 18, 2006, "this is the first time that shrimp have been exercised on a treadmill." To add weight to the shrimp as a means of increasing their stress level, Scholnick has made tiny backpacks out of duct tape.

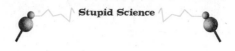

Return to Bedrock

A July 21, 2006, article in the *New York Times* reported that the Roche biotechnology company 454 Life Sciences and Germany's Max Planck Institute have made significant breakthroughs in mapping the genome of a Neanderthal man. The Neanderthal genome is a genetic sequence on one set of chromosomes that researchers claim has more than 99 percent similarity with that of *Homo sapiens*. In theory, the scientists claim, they could bring the species back to life by injecting the gene into a human egg, if only they could find a woman willing to carry a Neanderthal baby.

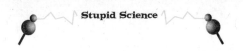
Egg-cellent

Finally, science has tackled the age-old problem of determining when an egg has been properly boiled soft, medium, or hard. The *Times* reported on July 31, 2006, that the British Egg Information Service announced the perfection and availability of the "smart egg." So throw away your old egg timer; the new "smart egg" has an invisible ink on the shell that turns black as soon as the egg is boiled just right.

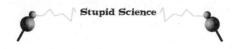

College Is a Real Blast

University of Nebraska chemistry professor John A. Belot, Jr., surprised his students by acting "bizarre," as if drunk, and by handing out several visual aids that turned out to be "homemade dynamite things or something," one student said. According to a September 11, 2006, article in the *Lincoln Journal Star*, police rounded up all the explosive devices Belot had passed around, and the professor was arrested and suspended with pay. Kirk Naylor, Belot's attorney, said the explosive situation has "been considerably blown out of proportion."

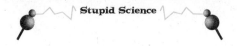

Growing Up Under a Microscope

Cleanliness may be next to godliness, but it might also lead to illness later in life, according to doctors in England. Reuters reported in a March 25, 1994, article that people who grow up in clean homes don't come into contact with small amounts of bacteria that might help immunize them from various illnesses such as Crohn's disease and ulcerative colitis.

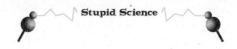
The Joke's on You

Researchers at Australia's University of New South Wales say they have discovered a diagnostic tool that can differentiate between people with Alzheimer's disease and those with frontotemporal dementia. What is the tool? Sarcasm. Head researcher John Hodges told the *Daily Telegraph* on December 14, 2008, that patients with Alzheimer's disease have no trouble understanding humor, but people with frontotemporal dementia just don't get it. "They are very bad at double meaning," Hodges said. "And a lot of humor is based on double meaning."

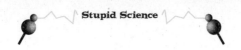

Wax On, Wax Off

Digging to find the gene for ear wax, researchers at Japan's Nagasaki University discovered that the ear wax of Africans and Europeans tends to be wetter, East Asians' wax is drier, and the moisture level of other Asians is right in the middle. But according to a January 30, 2006, article in the *New York Times*, they failed to uncover any other findings.

Geoffrey Miller, Joshua Tyber,
and Brent Jordan

won the

2008 Ig Nobel Prize
in

economics

for discovering that during peak fertility,
exotic dancers earn more money.

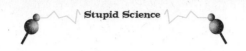

Wish It into the Cornfield, Anthony

While studying adolescents' reactions to brand names, professors at England's University of Bath discovered a startling amount of hatred and violence toward Mattel's Barbie doll. The *Times* reported on the researchers' findings in a December 19, 2005, article and divulged numerous accounts of torture and mutilation of Barbie, including the tearing off of limbs, scalping, burning, decapitation, and even microwaving.

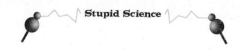

Don't Drink the Water

Seventh-grader Jasmine Roberts became famous at Benito Middle School when her hometown newspaper, the *Tampa Tribune*, published an article on February 13, 2006, announcing the findings of her award-winning science project. Twelve-year-old Jasmine discovered that ice from five local fast-food restaurants contained more bacteria (including *Escherichia coli*) than water from the same restaurants' toilets.

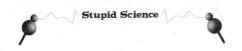

A Type of Science Foundation

Dr. Matthew Wright, a Southampton University (England) physicist, issued a report in the *International Journal of Clothing Science and Technology* stating that many women order the wrong size bra when shopping on the Internet. In his article "Graphical Analysis of Bra Size Calculation Procedures," Wright contends that shoppers commit a math error known as spurious rounding when converting rib cage and bust measurements to bra size. As noted in a December 9, 2002, article in the *Guardian*, Dr. Wright, an expert on acoustics, performed the research in his spare time.

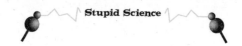
Make Sure It's Not Shinola

Sakae Shibusawa, an agricultural engineering professor at the Tokyo University of Agriculture and Technology, and his research team announced that by applying a combination of high pressure and intense heat to 5 pounds of cow poop, they were able to produce an ounce of gasoline, as reported by the Associated Press on March 3, 2006.

"Revenge Is Indeed Sweet, Study Finds"

Associated Press headline, August 27, 2004

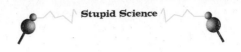
Karma Chameleon

Professor Greg Sotzing of the University of Connecticut at Storrs has developed threads of electrochromic polymers that can change color when an electric field is applied. Colored threads could be knitted into clothes with a number of thin conductive wires connected to a battery supply, and they could change color by means of a microcontroller. According to a *New Scientist* report from April 7, 2006, Sotzing said people could change the color of their clothes to suit their mood or to accessorize.

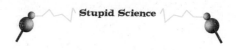

Up, Up, and Away

New Scientist magazine reported in an article dated May 15, 2006, that the Defense Advanced Research Projects Agency, an agency of the U.S. Department of Defense, was researching the possibility of a device similar to a cannon that would use human projectiles. The proposed use of the cannon would be to aim and launch special forces troops (and possibly firefighters and police officers) to land in specific locations on rocky terrain or difficult-to-reach locations such as rooftops.

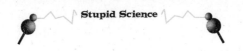

March of the Penguins

Numerous reports from the United Kingdom's Royal Air Force during the 1982 Falklands War stated that penguins would become so mesmerized by watching airplanes fly overhead that they would fall over backward. According to a BBC News report on February 2, 2001, British scientists conducted a five-week study into the pendulum penguin phenomenon and concluded that penguins don't lose their balance and fall over backward while watching low-flying aircraft. Now we can all rest a little easier.

"Earth Has Become Brighter, but No One Is Sure Why"

New York Times headline, May 6, 2005

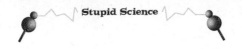

Waste Not, Want Not

As reported in an article in *New Scientist* (June 1, 2006), researchers at the University of Birmingham in the United Kingdom announced they had given chocolate waste to *Escherichia coli* (*E. coli*, as it's popularly known) bacteria, and they converted the sugar into hydrogen, which, in turn, powered a fuel cell. Researchers also claim that *E. coli* bacteria added to discarded automobile catalytic converters will leave behind, as waste, precious metals such as palladium, rhodium, and platinum.

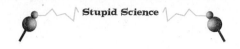
What's the Porpoise?

Dr. Hector Corona, an American scientist, published findings in 1996 that dolphins sing along to the radio. Corona claims that if you record dolphins and then play back the sounds they make at one-quarter speed, it seems as if they are singing pop songs. Apparently, the dolphins pick up radio sound waves from boats and other radios near the water and reproduce the tunes they hear. Corona claims that his dolphin recordings are renditions of hits from artists such as Mariah Carey and Bryan Adams, proving that although dolphins are intelligent, they don't have good taste.

"Inventor Creates Soundless Sound System"

USA Today headline, April 22, 2005

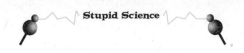

Vanilla Cow

Mayu Yamamoto, a researcher at the International Medical Center of Japan, was interviewed in a March 6, 2006, Agence France-Presse article and said her team had successfully extracted vanilla from ordinary cow excrement. Realizing that people are not going to eat vanilla extracted from cow poop, Yamamoto conceded that the flavoring could be used commercially only in nonconsumable products such as deodorants and shampoos.

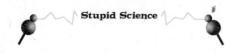

Designer Cats

On July 9, 2006, an article appeared in the *National Geographic News* about two companies preselling cats that have been genetically altered to be hypoallergenic. The San Diego firm Allerca Inc. is selling cats for $5,000 that have been created by cross-breeding species that lack the allergen known commonly as cat dander. Their main competitor, New York's Transgenic Pets, will be selling cats with modifications of the gene that produces the bacteria in their saliva for $1,000.

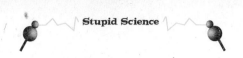

Money for Rope

What would you do if you were in a mental institution or prison where rope isn't allowed, but you desperately wanted to exercise by jumping rope? Well, an Associated Press article on May 31, 2006, reported that Lester Clancy had invented the solution: a ropeless jump rope. Clancy's invention is a pair of handles that replicate, electronically, the feel of an actual jump rope. No word on how one might play double Dutch.

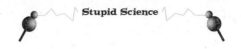
Because They're Both Small and Annoying

In November 2005, British inventor Howard Stapleton introduced a device called the Mosquito that emits an annoying high-frequency sound wave measuring about 17 kilohertz. Adolescents up to twenty years old can hear the sound, but people over thirty cannot. The device was created to dissuade unruly youths from hanging out in front of businesses without the side effect of repelling adult shoppers. According to a June 12, 2006, article in the *Times*, adolescents turned the tide on adults by downloading the high-frequency sound as a ring tone for their cell phones. That way, they can receive incoming calls and text messages without school officials knowing about it.

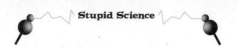

What's So Funny?

Shevach Friedler, an Israeli fertility specialist, reported at an international medical meeting in Prague, Czech Republic, that his research team had discovered that women are twice as successful with in vitro fertilization after having a brief encounter with clowns. Friedler, a trained mime, attributed the positive effects of clown interaction to stress reduction, according to a June 21, 2006, report by Reuters.

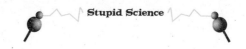

The Super Bowl of Science

"It's every man's dream to hear that beer and pizza can prevent cancer," said Dr. Richard Atkins of the National Prostate Cancer Coalition, commenting on research conducted at Oregon State University. It seems that xanthohumol, a micronutrient in beer, may reduce prostate cancer when combined with the previously known benefits of lycopene, which is found in tomatoes. The bad news, according to a June 13, 2006, Associated Press article, is that one would have to consume 120 beers and eat four large pizzas daily for the nutrients to have any effect. I'm sure there would be no lack of volunteers.

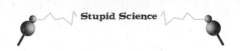

Missed It by That Much

The NASA Mars Climate *Orbiter* was launched on December 11, 1998, to study various weather and atmospheric conditions on Mars. As its name implies, the *Orbiter* was supposed to orbit Mars and radio information back to NASA. But the data in the software used to fire the thrusters and control the *Orbiter*'s rate of rotation were entered in U.S. measurement units when they were supposed to be in metric. The *Orbiter* missed its intended 140-kilometer (about 90-mile) altitude above Mars and instead entered the atmosphere at about 57 kilometers and burned up on September 23, 1999. The mistake cost not only invaluable information about Mars but also $327.6 million for both orbiter and lander (not including the miniature space probe, *Deep Space 2*).

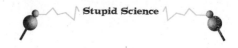

If You Can't Lick 'Em

The *Journal of the Federation of American Societies for Experimental Biology* reported in July 2008 that scientists from the Netherlands had discovered that histatin, a compound in human saliva, greatly speeds the healing of wounds. Observing that dogs lick their wounds to heal them, scientists now believe that histatin, which they previously thought only killed bacteria, can heal wounds in humans.

"Researcher Links Obesity, Food Portions"

Associated Press headline, January 3, 2004

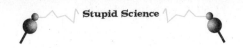

I'll Have an Atomic Fireball, Please

Scientist Hiroshi Watanabe, from the Japan Atomic Power Company in Takasaki, reported in December 1995 that irradiating cheap whiskey and wine with a fatal dose of gamma rays can improve the taste of the spirits. Watanabe also reported that ionizing good wine and whiskey with gamma rays makes them taste worse.

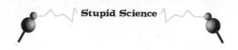

Aroma Therapy

Men, if you're trying to attract women with the smell of your cologne, you're in for a shock. According to Alan Hirsch of the Smell and Taste Treatment and Research Foundation of Chicago, Illinois, women are turned off by the smell of men's cologne, barbecued meat, and cherries. A March 11, 1998, article in the *Globe and Mail* of Toronto explained that Hirsch gauged the sexual arousal of research volunteers subjected to various smells. In case you're wondering, women are most turned on by the smell of baby powder, pumpkin pie, cucumbers, and lavender, but the smell that really gets them hot and bothered is Good 'n' Plenty candy.

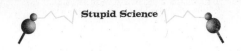

Keep It Down

A survey conducted by the Harvard School of Public Health in Cambridge, Massachusetts, and written up in a July 4, 2002, article in the *Boston Globe*, revealed that more people report noise and other public disturbances in neighborhoods surrounded by binge-drinking colleges than in other neighborhoods.

According to a January 7, 2008, article in the *Los Angeles Times*, Taser International introduced the Taser **MPH**, a combination neuromuscular incapacitation weapon and **MP3** music player.

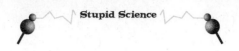

AC/DC

Beckman Research Institute, a research facility affiliated with the City of Hope National Medical Center in Duarte, California, announced in a September 16, 2002, article in *New Scientist* that they have genetically engineered flies to change their sexual orientation. Scientists revealed they were able to temporarily change the flies from heterosexual to homosexual simply by raising the external temperature to more than 86 degrees.

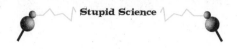

What Will the Neighbors Think?

Two Canadian astronomers beamed a twenty-three-page message into outer space in hopes that it will help alien life forms understand the human race and our level of intelligence. But in June 1999, a month after the signal was sent, the astronomers admitted they had made a mistake. A portion of the message that shows how humans have evolved in their understanding of mathematics used two different "equals" symbols. The Dutch researcher who originally uncovered the mistake was disheartened, believing that aliens will think Earthlings are "a sloppy species."

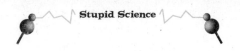

Über Mouse

By modifying a single metabolism gene in mice, researchers led by Richard Hanson of Case Western Reserve University in Cleveland, Ohio, have produced a race of supermice. The *Independent* reported on November 5, 2007, that the mice are genetically enhanced to use stored body fat as energy and can run five hours nonstop. They live longer and have three times as much sexual activity as regular mice. Although Hanson admitted the same alteration could give us a race of supermen and superwomen, "This is not something that you'd do to a human. It's completely wrong."

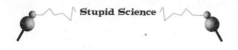

Live Long and Prosper

According to a November 25, 1995, article in the *Economist*, inventor Yoshiro Nakamatsu of Japan documented and photographed every meal he ate for the past thirty years as research for his Yummi Nutri Brain biscuits. Nakamatsu used the data to discover which "brain foods" would go into his biscuits to help make people smarter and (with the addition of exercise and sex) stretch life expectancy to 144 years. In order to help in the exercise and sex department, Nakamatsu also invented spring-loaded jogging shoes and a sex toy called the Love-Jet.

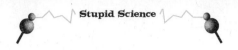

Cooking with Gas

Canadian newspaper the *Globe and Mail* reported in a June 14, 1994, article that New Delhi, India, had produced enough gas to fuel streetlights and provide cooking fuel for approximately thirty families. The energy, they reported, was derived from human waste collected from nearly forty of their city's public toilets.

This Is Only a (Science) Test
#3

The following are actual answers to questions
on science exams.

Q: What happens to a boy when he reaches puberty?

A: He says good-bye to his boyhood and looks
forward to his adultery.

Q: Name a major disease associated with cigarettes.

A: Premature death.

Q: What is artificial insemination?

A: When the farmer does it to the bull instead
of the cow.

Q: How are the main parts of the body categorized
(e.g., abdomen)?

A: The body is consisted into three parts: the
brainium, the borax and the abdominal cavity. The
brainium contains the brain; the borax contains
the heart and lungs, and the abdominal cavity
contains the five bowels, A, E, I, O, and U.

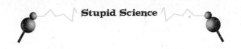

Getting into a Real Jam

Researchers from Humboldt State University in California reported in the *Dallas Morning News* (August 7, 1995) that they had discovered chemical compounds that can kill several common types of bacteria, such as *Propionibacterium acnes* (which causes acne), and certain fungi (including one that causes athlete's foot). The researchers discovered this naturally occurring chemical in the toe jam of black-tailed deer.

Đorian Raymer and Đouglas Smith

won the

2008 Ig Nobel Prize

in

physics

*for proving that clumps of string
or hair will inevitably tangle.*

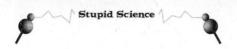

Robo-Roach

To better understand the social habits of cockroaches, a research team from the Free University of Brussels, Belgium, created tiny cockroach robots. The roach-bots were treated with cockroach pheromones and released into a nest of cockroaches to see whether they could influence behavior. It was discovered that some of the real cockroaches followed the robots into a sunny area, although cockroaches don't usually like light, according to a November 16, 2007, article in the *Canadian Press*. However, despite being programmed, more than half of the robots were lulled into a "spell" by the real cockroaches and followed them into shaded areas.

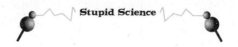

Beer Goggles

Barry Jones, a psychology professor at Scotland's Glasgow University, conducted research on alcohol's effect on perception and discovered, oddly enough, that after three beers both men and women found members of the opposite sex more attractive. The study, reported in an August 19, 2002, Reuters article, revealed that perceived attractiveness was 25 percent higher after the beers than before them.

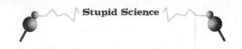

When You Gotta Glow, You Gotta Glow

By genetically modifying an aquarium-kept zebrafish with DNA from a jellyfish, scientists at Taiwan's Taikong Corporation were able to make the tropical fish glow yellow and green, according to a June 15, 2003, article in the *Observer*.

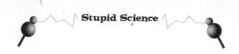
Soylent Green

With a combined effort from various labs in the United States, Australia, and the Netherlands, scientists have been able to grow frog and mouse meat in the lab and are now tackling chicken, pork, and beef. Toronto's *Globe and Mail* announced on March 27, 2006, that scientists hope to develop an industrial version of their meat-growing process within the next five years. The meat would resemble natural meat in texture and flavor but could be engineered to be as healthful as salmon. Interest in the process has already spread, with one private group expressing a desire to grow human meat. They admitted that finding funding for such work would be problematic.

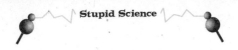
Your Pad or Mine?

The BBC reported on June 30, 1999, about some interesting work volunteers performed at Philadelphia's Monell Chemical Senses Center that year. It was revealed that volunteers were required to sniff underarm pads and express their reaction to the odor. For example, most volunteers could tell by sniffing underarm pads whether they were from happy people or fearful people. It was also noted that sniffing underarm pads from older women made the volunteers feel happy, whereas inhaling the fumes from the pads of young men caused sadness and melancholy.

Thomas Edison was afraid of the dark.

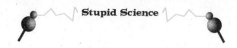

Don't Make a Monkey out of Me

Texas Tech biology professor Michael Dini was placed under investigation by the U.S. Department of Justice, according to a February 3, 2002, *New York Times* article, after students complained about his policies. Apparently, Dini will give students a letter of recommendation only if they tell him they don't believe in creationism and that they firmly believe in evolution.

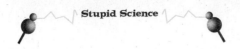

Cat Got Your Tongue

A researcher writing in the January–February issue of
Australasian Science magazine, as reported in a December 26,
2006, article in the Australian Associated Press, reported that
the *Toxoplasma gondii* protozoan, whose primary host is the
domestic cat, does more than harm the fetus of pregnant
women. Their report concluded that toxoplasmosis also could
lower IQs in men and make women more promiscuous.

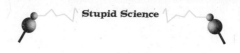

Defy the Law of Gravity

Inventor Joseph Thompson of the United Kingdom is angry with the Patents, Designs and Trademarks office because it refused his application for a patent on a flying saucer, citing the fact that his design violates two laws of physics. The office refused Thompson's application for a patent for three years, and an appeals court agreed with their decision: "There would be, if Mr. Thompson's device were to work, a fundamental change in the currently understood laws of physics," said Lord Justice Jacob. According to a June 22, 2006, article in the *Manchester Evening News*, the court sympathized with Thompson's plight and said if he built a working model of his saucer, they would reconsider his patent application.

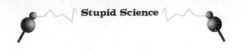

These Guys Are Nuts

According to a March 20, 2003, Canadian Broadcasting Corporation news report, the government of Ontario came under criticism after it gave a grant of $150,000 Canadian dollars (U.S. $135,000) to researchers at Laurentian University. The grant helped fund a project whose purpose was to study how wildlife adapts to the environment by examining, in detail, the sex drives of squirrels.

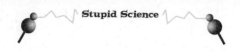

I Am Air-Ace, Bluebottle

As reported in a June 4, 2008, Agence France-Presse article, scientists at Switzerland's University of Lausanne who studied the evolution of ordinary houseflies over the course of thirty to forty generations concluded that flies tend to live longer if they're stupid. The researchers postulated that intelligent flies might overtax their biological systems.

The little lump of flesh in front of the entrance to your ear canal is called a tragus.

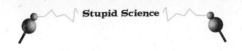

Totally Awesome, Dude!

Believe it or not, random number generators on computers don't really generate random numbers; because all computers follow a set of programmed functions, it's impossible for them to be truly random. But scientists have discovered something that does produce random numbers: a lava lamp. In their article "Method for Seeding a Pseudo-random Number Generator with a Cryptographic Hash of a Digitization of a Chaotic System," published on March 24, 1998, Robert G. Mende, Jr., Landon Curt Noll, and Sanjeev Sisodiya showed that by using an array of six lava lamps in front of a digital camera, they can produce truly random numbers. Mende claims the inspiration for the project came to him one afternoon while he "was avoiding work."

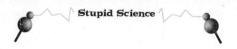

Rocket J. Squirrel

A presentation at the International Society for Behavioral Ecology in Ithaca, New York, by Jane Waterman, an ecologist at the University of Central Florida, praised the lascivious and debased mating habits of male South African squirrels. Waterman explained the rodents' "love 'em and leave 'em" attitude and attributed their behavior to the fact that "they're hung." *New Scientist* reported on the conference in their August 15, 2008, edition and explained that if you compared the squirrels proportionally to humans, you'd be looking at a penis 13 inches long.

"Official Statistics Say Don't Trust Official Statistics"

Lancashire (England) *Evening Post* headline, March 18, 2008

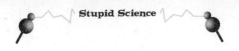

Science Classic

As part of a 1971 experiment to study the effects and causes of landslides, Japanese scientists watered down a hill using fire hoses to simulate the effect of a torrential rainstorm. The soil on the hill gave way under the enormous amount of water, and the resulting landslide killed four scientists and eleven observers.

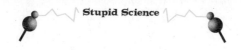

What's the Square Root of Roundworms?

A July 3, 2008, article in *Science Daily* reported on a research article in *Nature* from a team of University of Oregon biologists studying roundworms. Their findings indicated that in order to find food or avoid trouble, roundworms do calculus-type computations using neurons capable of sensing various chemicals (chemosensory neurons).

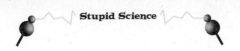

Tit for Tat

In a reversal of the sexist phrase "size does matter," a female researcher at the University of Central Florida revealed that men found women with C-cup breasts more professional than women with larger or smaller bosoms, according to a March 17, 2001, article in the *Atlanta Journal-Constitution*.

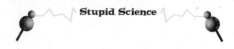

Dense and Density

Research conducted at the Hebrew Rehabilitation Center in Boston, Massachusetts, revealed that one major reason men suffer less osteoporosis (a reduction in bone mineral density) than women is that they drink more beer. Dr. Douglas Kiel found that barley, a grain in beer, contains the mineral silicon, which helps strengthen bones. Because of their greater beer consumption, men get up to 33 percent more silicon in their diet than women. In short, according to the July 4, 2002, *American Journal of Clinical Nutrition* report, beer builds better bones.

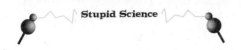

I'll Be a Monkey's Uncle

Lawyer Steven Wise, promoting his book *Drawing the Line: Science and the Case for Animal Rights* at a Washington, D.C., bookstore, told audience members that because some animals experience emotions, use language, and interact socially, "I don't see a difference between a chimpanzee and my 4½-year-old son," based on the fact that "chimps have 98 percent of DNA in common with humans." The *Toronto Star* reported on June 15, 2002, that Wise's son Christopher was not in the audience and was therefore unavailable for comment.

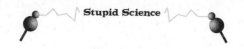

Sex Doesn't Always Sell

On June 30, 2002, the *Miami Herald* reported on a study conducted at Iowa State University that showed that it was more difficult for viewers to remember commercials that were aired during shows containing explicit sex scenes than during other types of television programs.

Now Donald Feels Goofy

Professor Trevor Cox from the University of Salford in England, his team of fellow acoustic researchers, and a duck named Daisy debunked once and for all the myth that a duck's quack doesn't have an echo. The *Guardian* reported on Cox's acoustic experiments with Daisy in a September 8, 2003, article in which the professor stated that the origin of the myth could be that "a duck quacks rather quietly, so the sound coming back is at a low level and might not be heard." Cox explained that another reason is that ducks are normally found in open water areas and are seldom found quacking around echoing cliffs.

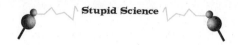

Let's Give That Man a Hand

According to an October 24, 2003, Associated Press article, biologist Nette Levermann of Copenhagen's Zoological Museum, along with his research team, monitored one hundred walruses off the coast of Greenland and reported that the large mammals use their right flippers more than their left.

"Why Pregnant Women Don't Tip Over"

New York Times headline, December 12, 2007

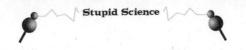

What's That You're Wearing?

As reported in a July 2, 2007, article in *New Scientist*, researchers at the University of Calgary subjected female mice to the
odor of male mouse pheromones to gauge their reaction.
Scientists expected to see heightened sexual arousal, but in
addition, the scent apparently made the brains of the female
mice grow larger.

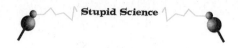

Drat, Said the Rat

An article in the *Journal of Agricultural and Food Chemistry*, also reported in the January 19, 2005, issue of *New Scientist*, showed that rates of DNA-damaging cancers caused by heterocyclic amines, a carcinogen found in cooked meat, were higher in rats that drank nonalcoholic beer than in rats that drank water.

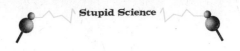

Eating Like a Pig

Researchers at the University of Guelph in Ontario, Canada, reported in 2001 that they had developed a new breed of Yorkshire pigs called Enviropigs that use plant phosphorus more efficiently. The genetically enhanced porkers are able to more effectively digest phytate, a phosphate found in their cereal grain diet, thereby eliminating the need to supplement the pigs' diet with phosphate or phytase enzymes. Farmers usually include phosphate in pig slop to foster optimal growth and development.

Marie-Christine Cadiergues,
Christel Joubert, and Michel Franc

won the

2008 Ig Nobel Prize

in

biology

for proving that fleas that live on dogs are
higher jumpers than fleas that live on cats.

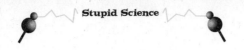

Toe the Line

Irina Stepanov, a researcher at the University of Minnesota Cancer Center, reported in a December 28, 2006, article on the university's Web site that she found the tobacco smoke–related carcinogen nicotine-derived nitrosamine ketone in toenail clippings not only from smokers but also from nonsmokers exposed to second-hand smoke.

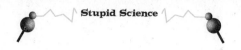

This Jelly Tastes Weird

Using layers of cells that mimic skin, Stephen Britland at the University of Bradford in the United Kingdom and his colleagues discovered that wounds healed faster after they applied extracts of maggot juice to them. *New Scientist* reported on Britland's experiments on October 9, 2006, and noted that the team had already created a prototype maggot jelly that works just as effectively as directly applying live maggots.

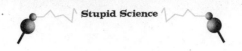

A Slippery Slope

Dimitra Dodou from Delft University of Technology in the Netherlands received her Ph.D. for her research into creating a robot that can glide through the sensitive colon without damaging the delicate walls. *ScienceDaily* reported on Dodou's invention in the September 25, 2006, issue and explained how her tiny mucus-riding robot might change the way colonoscopies are performed.

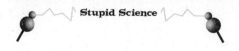
A Hot (News) Flash

Researchers at Chicago's Brookfield Zoo documented the fact that not only do human females experience menopause, but so do female gorillas, according to a report on NationalGeographic.com (December 27, 2005).

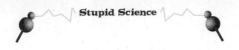
Depressing Results

Seasonal affective disorder, also known as the winter blues, is a mood disorder commonly associated with a lack of sunlight. Researchers at Ohio State University began a project to see whether hamsters also suffer from the disorder, according to a January 10, 2005, *Columbus Dispatch* article.

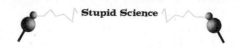

Catch-as Catch-Can

The Norwegian newspaper *Verdens Gang* ran a series on unusual summer jobs in their June 25, 2003, edition that included Svein Tore Hauge's employment. His job consists of following cows around and catching their poop in a container before it hits the ground. Scientists at Saerheim Plant Research, where Hauge works, want "pristine" dung for their research, so the feces must be free of grass, dirt, and foreign bacteria. Collecting the samples is usually easy, said Hauge, but "sometimes it just sprays in all directions."

The average person passes nearly a pint of intestinal gas every day by flatulence.

Better Than a Rabbit's Foot

Dr. Anthony Atala, director of the Institute for Regenerative Medicine at Wake Forest Baptist Medical Center in Winston-Salem, North Carolina, announced on May 23, 2006, at the annual meeting of the American Urological Association that he had grown an artificial penis from a rabbit. Atala said he was able to re-create a fully functional penis using the rabbit's own genes and that everything worked like a charm.

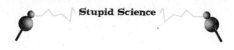

Cowabunga, Dude!

AmBreed New Zealand Limited, which specializes in breeding services and equipment for livestock, has effectively eliminated the old-fashioned method ranchers use to manually gather sperm from bulls. According to a June 14, 2006, Reuters article, the company introduced a fake "cow," a small go-kart with natural cowhide on its roof, which the bull mounts. The driver of the cow-kart waits until the bull has had its way with the bogus Bessie and then drives away with a full load.

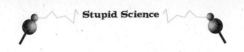

Taming of the Shrew

Microbiologists writing in the July 2008 issue of the official journal of the U.S. National Academy of Sciences reported that the Malaysian pen-tailed tree shrew could be considered the frat boy of the animal kingdom. The animal drinks fermented nectar from flower buds of the bertam palm plant, which can reach up to a 3.8 percent alcohol content (the equivalent of most light beers), and doesn't get drunk. "The amount of alcohol we're talking about is huge," said researcher Marc-André Lachance, a microbiologist at the University of Western Ontario. "It's several times the legal limit in most countries."

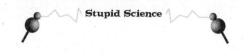

Cut Him Off at the Past

University of Connecticut physics professor Ronald Mallett has dreamed of going back in time to when he was ten years old to warn his father of the dangers of smoking. According to an April 5, 2002, article in the *Boston Globe*, Mallett began experimenting on genuine time travel involving no more than a neutron or two. He based his research on Einstein's theory of special relativity but doesn't believe the technology is currently available to produce the amount of energy needed for a human to go back in time.

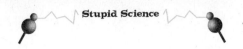

What's Good for the Goose

There are two current theories on why women earn less money than men. One is simple gender discrimination; the other is that women put more emphasis on family and are less career-oriented than men. According to a report in the October 10, 2008, issue of *Time* magazine, the current *Journal of Economic Analysis and Policy* promotes the former theory. A study of career women who underwent a sex change showed that they increased their earnings slightly, whereas the salaries of men who had a sex change dropped by about one third.

The jiffy is an actual unit of time.
It's equal to 3.3357×10^{-11} seconds, or
the length of time it takes light
to travel one centimeter in
a vacuum.

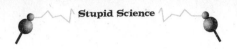

Making a Monkey out of Wasps

Charles Darwin, best known for his groundbreaking and perpetually controversial book *On the Origin of Species*, later wrote an interesting book called *The Various Contrivances by Which Orchids Are Fertilized by Insects*. Building off this research, according to a July 15, 2008, article in the *New York Times*, Australian biologists documented a group of very tricky orchids that fool male insects by acquiring the look and smell of female wasps to entice the wasp to pollinate them. The authors of the research theorized that because female wasps can reproduce with or without sperm (self-propagation always creates male offspring), the plant might be adopting Darwin's survival of the fittest by creating more males and thereby increasing the number of future pollinators.

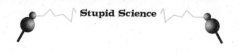

Clam Chowder

Biologist Peter Fong was happier than a clam when he stumbled on something that made clams, well, happy as clams. Fong, from Pennsylvania's Gettysburg College, was doing research on the nervous system of fingernail clams when he decided to see how they reacted when he put the antidepressant Prozac into the water. The *New York Times* reported on his experiment in an article on February 17, 1998, and noted that after the introduction of Prozac, the clams started reproducing at ten times their normal rate.

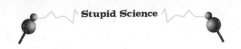
Anesthesiologists Aren't the Only Ones Who Pass Gas

The old saying "He who smelt it dealt it" doesn't always apply, especially if you're dealing with groggy patients after major surgery. That's why Mitreben Laboratories, in partnership with Osaka Railway Hospital, developed a machine that can detect gaseous emissions from patients; in other words, it's a fancy fart detector. Japan's *Shukan Shincho* magazine reported on March 22, 2001, about the *hohi kenshutsuki* machine, which lets doctors know when a patient's bowels have begun to move after surgery.

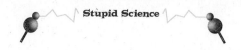

Slower Than Molasses

Professor Thomas Parnell started an experiment in 1927, and although he died in 1947, the experiment still continues. Parnell wanted to prove that pitch is fluid, not solid, and he constructed an hourglass-like apparatus that allows the pitch to drip slowly—and I mean slowly. The first drop fell in 1938, the second was seen in 1947, the third in 1954. Drips were then noted in 1962, 1970, 1979, and 1988, with the last drop falling on November 28, 2000. Scientists estimate that the next drop could fall anytime between 2009 and 2012, according to an October 7, 2005, report on the University of Queensland (Brisbane, Australia) Web site.

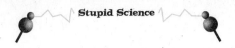

Getting a Snootful

Pig farms smell bad, there's no doubt about that, but during the International Round Table on Swine Odor Control, held in Ames, Iowa, in May 1994, more than one hundred scientists examined this simple fact in detail. Presenters included a firm that sells electronic equipment to measure the level of odor offensiveness and a researcher who revealed that neighbors who lived downwind of a large hog farm in North Carolina reacted to the smell by becoming "tense, depressed, angry, and confused." Said one scientist, "We're dealing with complex issues that don't just come down to 'does it smell bad?'"

"Arctic Ice Melts Faster
as It Gets Warmer"

Associated Press headline, September 29, 2005

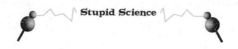

Green Jelly Genes

Jellyfish have genes that make them glow green, and scientists have been tinkering with ways to use that unique phenomenon in other plants and animals. In June 1999 the Scottish Agricultural College created a potato that glows green when it needs water. And Hertfordshire University in England announced in October 1999 that it would genetically alter Douglas spruce trees with jellyfish genes in order to create naturally illuminating Christmas trees.

Scientists are also using firefly genes in a similar process, according to research conducted in December 1999 at the University of Cincinnati. They will produce self-lighting Christmas trees and zebrafish that glow when they detect certain pollutants in water.

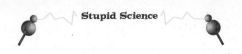

The Backside Blasters

Penguins are known as the super-poopers of the animal kingdom because of the force with which they expel their feces. Victor Benno Meyer-Rochow and Jozsef Gal of the International University Bremen in Germany conducted research into the pooping power of penguins, and they estimate that the birds generate pressures of up to 60 kilopascals—more than half normal atmospheric pressure and more than four times the peak squeeze typically exerted by humans. The penguins catapult their crap in order to avoid messing up their feathers and nest, according to *New Scientist* in January 10, 2005.

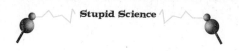

Picky Research

Habitually picking your nose is not a problem for most people, but two Wisconsin researchers, writing in the February 1995 *Journal of Clinical Psychiatry*, have concluded that a small percentage of the population "may meet criteria for a disorder—rhinotillexomania." Their survey of 1,000 randomly selected adults, gathering 254 respondents, found that 66.4 percent did it "to relieve discomfort or itchiness," 2.1 percent did it for "enjoyment," and 0.4 percent did it for "sexual stimulation." The majority of respondents (65.1 percent) used their index finger, 20.2 percent used their pinkie finger, and 16.4 percent used their thumb. "Once removed, the nasal debris was examined, at least some of the time, by most respondents"; no word on whether they conducted taste tests.

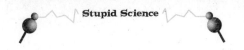

What's in Your Genes?

In December 2002, the U.S. Defense Advanced Research Projects Agency (DARPA) announced the Odortype Detection Program and offered scientists $3.2 million to discover a genetic odor fingerprint unique to every individual. The proposal stated that DARPA is "soliciting innovative proposals to (1) determine whether genetically-determined odortypes can be used to identify specific individuals, and if so (2) to develop the science and enabling technology for detecting and identifying specific individuals by such odortypes." Big Brother is sniffing you!

"Pessimism Raises Dementia Risk, Study Finds"

Reuters headline, April 15, 2005

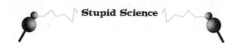

Some Like It Hot

Entomologist Grady Glenn of Texas A&M University discovered that termites don't like their wood splinters spicy. Glenn's research concluded that habanero capsaicin, a component of the chili pepper, acts as a deterrent to termites. Glenn treated wood samples with various substances and studied the reaction from termites, according to an August 20, 1999, Associated Press article, when he hit upon the heat factor. The habanero pepper is sixty times hotter than the jalapeño and ten times hotter than cayenne. "Pretty quickly they learned which end of the wood had habanero," Glenn said. "I don't blame them."

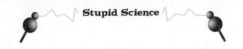
What the Flock Are You Looking At?

"If they can do that with faces, the implication is that they have to have reasonable intelligence, otherwise what is the point of having a system for remembering faces and not remembering anything else?" asked behavioral scientist Keith Kendrick from the Babraham Institute in Cambridge, England. Sheep, which are usually considered quite dim, actually have a very keen memory and can recognize as many as fifty other sheep for up to two years, according to an article in the November 7, 2001, issue of *National Geographic Today*. "It is a very sophisticated memory system," Kendrick said. "They are showing similar abilities in many ways to humans." Which isn't anything the sheep should be too proud of.

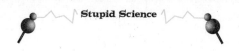

Rave Reviews

Scientists from Cambridge University drugged 238 mice with various amphetamines and subjected them to loud dance or classical music to gauge the results. Of the forty mice injected with methamphetamine and forced to listen to music by the dance group The Prodigy at very high volume, seven died. Of the mice forced to listen to Bach's "Violin Concerto in A Minor," which has a similar tempo, four died as a result. The conclusion, according to a November 1, 2001, BBC News report, was that loud music somehow strengthens the effects of methamphetamine in animals. There was no mention of whether glow sticks were involved.

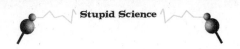
Looking Up to Someone

"Tallness is pretty much universally attractive," says researcher Allan Mazur from New York's Syracuse University, as quoted in a May 9, 2001, article in *New Scientist*. Mazur says he does not know why this is true even after working with a team of scientists from the University of Marburg, Germany. Their combined research revealed that tall men tend to father more children (from different women), and they speculated that this is because they are more attractive and have more extramarital affairs, which leads to more offspring. "The more attractive a man is, the more chance he gets to destroy his first marriage," Mazur concluded.

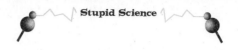

A Strain of Stain Removers

We've got self-cleaning ovens, so why not self-cleaning clothes? Well, biotechnologists at the University of Massachusetts must have thought the same thing. According to a July 5, 2001, article in *New Scientist*, researchers are looking into implanting fibers with a strain of *Escherichia coli* bacteria that will eat human sweat and dirt. If your clothes are clean, you can reactivate the bacteria with nutrients; basically, you'll have to feed your clothes in order to keep them clean or just wear them until they become dirty again.

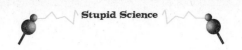

Why the Big Reaction?

Researchers at Japan's Central Research Institute of Electrical Power Industry, funded by the Japan Atomic Energy Research Institute, began studies of the feasibility of using miniature nuclear reactors, the size of a broom closet, as a power source for offices and apartment buildings in densely packed Tokyo. According to an August 22, 2001, article in *New Scientist*, the reactor developed by Toshiba Corporation, called the Rapid-L, was originally designed as a lunar-based power station.

"Louis Pasteur's theory of germs is ridiculous fiction."

Pierre Pachet, professor of physiology at Toulouse, 1872

ALL IN A DAY'S WORK

Popular Science's "10 Worst Jobs in Science" for 2007 included the following:

- Rosalind Rolland, a senior researcher at the New England Aquarium in Boston who heads a team of whale feces researchers. "It surprised even me how much you can learn about a whale through its feces," she was quoted as saying.

- Neal Haskell, one of the nation's leading forensic entomologists, who studies maggot-infested human corpses.

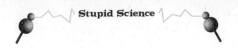

Pigging Out on Junk Food

Researchers from Ohio State University fed barbecue-flavored and sour cream–flavored potato chips, which are nearly 33 percent fat, to 250 pigs to see what impact they would have on their eating habits. Surprisingly, because of the salt and fat content of the chips, the pigs ate less than their usual portion of feed, thereby delaying their optimal growth by two weeks. The upside is that although the pigs didn't become as fat, after they were killed and cooked their meat was declared juicer and tastier, according to an August 9, 1998, Associated Press article, with no potato chip aftertaste.

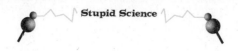

Spreading It Around

Everyone knows that sneezing spreads germs, and that's why we're supposed to cover our mouths. But researchers in Sydney, Australia, wanted to find out whether farting also spreads germs. According to the June 29, 2001, issue of *New Scientist*, scientists asked a boy to pass gas on a laboratory dish. Dr. Karl Kruszelnicki announced that the next morning bacteria were found growing all over the plate and that his team would continue experimenting by conducting "tests [that] involve breaking wind on to lab plates from varying distances after having specific foods and drinks."

This Is Only a (Science) Test
#4

The following are actual answers to questions
on science exams.

Q: What is the fibula?

A: *A small lie.*

Q: What does "varicose" mean?

A: *Nearby.*

Q: Give the meaning of the term "caesarean
section."

A: *The Caesarean Section is a district in Rome.*

Q: What does the word "benign" mean?

A: *Benign is what you will be after you be eight.*

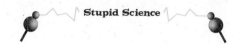

Don't Have a Cow, Man

Professor José Antonio Visintin, of the Department of Animal Reproduction of the School of Veterinary Medicine and Zootechny of the University of São Paulo in Brazil, and his team attempted to clone the first cow, but the results weren't what they expected: They ended up with an ox. Visintin had two possible explanations for what happened, according to an April 30, 2002, article from Ananova. Either a lab assistant accidentally impregnated the cow with an ox embryo, or as Visintin said, "She must have cheated on us!"

"Everything that can be invented has been invented."

Charles H. Duell, commissioner, U.S. Office of Patents, 1899

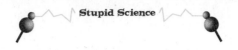

Passive Restraint

In the movie *Armageddon*, a group of ragtag astronauts led by Bruce Willis blow up an asteroid on a collision course with Earth. But scientist Hermann Burchard of Oklahoma State University in Stillwater told *New Scientist* magazine on August 29, 2002, that he has a better idea: Use a giant airbag instead. Burchard believes spacecraft flying alongside the celestial object could inflate a "billowing space pillow" several miles wide and nudge the threatening object off its course. Burchard believes his idea to be "safe, simple, and realistic" but admits there are a few details he hasn't worked out yet.

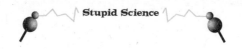

Laptops: Still a Hot Item

If you're a member of the computer laptop community, you'll be interested in the story of a laptop that burned one of its members: the member belonging to an unnamed fifty-year-old scientist. Claes-Göran Östenson of the Karolinska Institute in Sweden wrote in a letter published in *Lancet* on November 22, 2002, about a father of two whose prolonged laptop use burned his penis. "The ventral part of his scrotal skin had turned red, and there was a blister with a diameter of about two centimeters (0.8 inches)," Östenson wrote. In case you're wondering, the scientist claimed to have been wearing both underwear and trousers while he worked on his laptop for more than an hour.

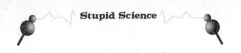

Whiter Shade of Pale

In January 2002, Ivan Baldry and Karl Glazebrook of Johns Hopkins University in Maryland postulated that if the universe were viewed from a great distance, it would appear turquoise. But in a June 26, 2002, article from Reuters, the researchers admitted they had used the wrong shade of white in their data and now claim that the universe is beige. Glazebrook told *New Scientist*, "I'm very embarrassed. I don't like being wrong."

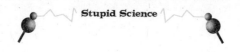

S.O.S.

"The water activity of the different sandwich components needs to complement each other," project officer Michelle Richardson told *New Scientist* magazine on April 12, 2002. "If the water activity of the meat is too high you might get soggy bread." This gave Richardson's team at the Army Soldier Systems Center in Massachusetts the impetus to create a vacuum-sealed sandwich that uses chemicals to inhibit bacterial growth and has a shelf life of up to three years. Their success with the nonsoggy sandwich has spurred them to continue their experiments with pizzas, bagels, burritos, and even peanut butter and jelly.

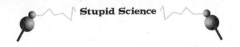

John Crapper Would Be Proud

People have been urinating as long as the human race has existed, but apparently most of us are still doing it incorrectly. According to an August 12, 2002, article on News.com, Australian scientist Ajay Rane says the proper way to pee for both men and women is "to sit on the toilet with their feet flat on the ground, elbows on their knees, and leaning forward as if they're reading a newspaper on the floor." The James Cook University professor has spent years trying to help people who suffer from weak bladders and says this posture "improves both bladder and bowel function." He's now studying whether sitting toilets or squatting toilets are best for bowel and bladder evacuation.

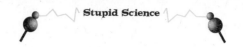
Only Innies Need Apply

Karl Kruszelnicki, a researcher at the University of Sydney, Australia, studied samples of bellybutton lint submitted by five thousand volunteers to determine its makeup. Kruszelnicki discovered that the lint is a combination of skin cells and clothing fibers that are directed to the navel by body hair "as all roads lead to Rome." The Associated Press reported on Kruszelnicki's findings in an article on October 4, 2002, and quoted him as saying, "Your typical generator of bellybutton lint or fluff is a slightly overweight, middle-aged male with a hairy abdomen."

"Gas-Pumping Robot: What Could Go Wrong?"

Reuters headline, February 4, 2008

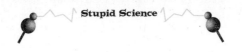

Fartosaurus Rex

It's one of the mysteries of science: What caused the dinosaurs to become extinct? Most scientists believe it was a planetary catastrophe or a comet or asteroid impact, but one French scientist proposed that flatulence killed the dinosaurs. According to a July 28, 2000, BBC News report, the scientist said, "The animals, weighing from eighty to 100 tonnes, would eat on average between 130 and 260 kilos of food every day. They would fart non-stop." He went on to speculate that the atmosphere became charged with methane, which damaged the ozone layer. Basically, what scientists are warning us about now concerning cow flatulence and global warming.

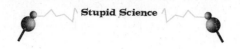

Pamela Anderson—Maybe

Faculty and administrators at middle schools in Kanawha County, West Virginia, were criticized for continuing to use science textbooks that have a multitude of erroneous entries, according to a January 14, 2001, Associated Press article. Among the errors cited in the Prentice Hall science textbook series was a photograph of singer Linda Ronstadt with the caption, "A silicon crystal."

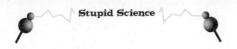

Money for Nothing

Paleontologist Scott Sampson discovered a previously unknown dinosaur during a dig in Madagascar, and because his
team had been listening to the British rock group Dire Straits
at the time, he decided to name the creature *Masiakasaurus
knopfleri*, after lead singer Mark Knopfler. The name of the
newly discovered dinosaur, a small predatory theropod whose
front teeth projected forward instead of straight down, is
derived from *masiaka* (Malagasy for "vicious") and *sauros*
(Greek for "lizard"). According to the January 2001 issue of
Nature magazine, the name literally translates to "'vicious
lizard of Knopfler."

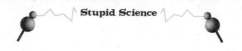

The Heart of the Matter

The *American Journal of Cardiology* reported in March 2005 that the survival rate after coronary artery bypass grafting (a type of cardiac bypass surgery) is greater in overweight patients than nonoverweight patients.

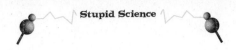

Our Overly Litigious Society

In the April 15, 2003, issue of *New Scientist* magazine, the editors noticed that Bell's Antiseptic Cream included the following warning on the product: "Avoid contact with eyes, ears, brain and surrounding membrane. Do not use in body cavities or as an enema." In the article, the editors wrote, "[One] wonders whether anyone who is attracted to the idea of drilling holes in their skull and smearing cream on their brain while giving themselves an antiseptic cream enema would be capable of understanding this warning anyway."

"U.S. Losing Lead in Science and Engineering: Study"

Reuters headline, July 10, 2005

"Allegations of Fake Research Hit New High"

Associated Press headline, July 12, 2005

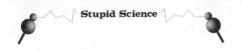
Go, Go, Gadget Pigeon

The Central Intelligence Agency's Science and Technology Directorate, located in its headquarters near Washington, D.C., celebrated its fortieth anniversary by revealing a few of its secret wartime gadgets, according to a December 26, 2003, Associated Press article. One was a miniature surveillance camera mounted on the back of a pigeon. Unfortunately, even though the camera was small, it was still too heavy to allow the pigeon to fly, and it had to walk home.

Another invention was a listening device, to be hidden in the Asian jungles, that was disguised to look like tiger droppings.

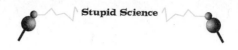

I Thought You Said It Was Pea Soup

It might be true that an army moves on its stomach, but the latest invention in the field of dehydrated foodstuffs is sure to turn the stomach of even the strongest soldier. According to a July 24, 2004, article in *New Scientist*, a U.S. Army laboratory in Natick, Massachusetts, has developed a lightweight, dried ration that can be safely hydrated with nearly any kind of liquid, including filthy swamp water or a soldier's own urine. A perforated membrane over the food filters out 99.9 percent of any bacteria, chemicals, or other contaminants and allows only water molecules to pass. Although it will work, urine is recommended only as a last resort because the membrane won't filter out uric acid, which could build up and cause damage in a soldier's kidneys.

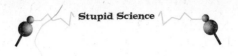
What a Croc

Scientists believe that crocodiles rely, in part, on the earth's magnetic fields to navigate. Therefore, Florida wildlife managers began an experiment to keep crocs from returning to residential neighborhoods by temporarily taping magnets to their heads. Their hope is that the magnets will disrupt the crocodiles' homing ability, said Lindsey Hord, crocodile response coordinator for the Florida Fish and Wildlife Conservation Commission. And according to a February 25, 2009, Reuters article, it really is a hope. "Hey, we might as well give this a try," Hord remarked.

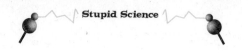

I Thought They Were Shy

British scientists were honored with the 2002 Ig Nobel Prize for their research into the reproductive habits of the ostrich. Their observations uncovered that ostriches became more sexually aroused when a human was present; in fact, some ostriches tried to become amorous with the human observers.

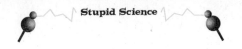

That Really Bites

In the June 17, 1999, issue of the *New England Journal of Medicine*, in their article "Envenomations by Rattlesnakes Thought to Be Dead," two doctors reported on a 1972 study showing that rattlesnake heads are dangerous for twenty to sixty minutes after decapitation. Their research showed that "young men—particularly while intoxicated—suffer a disproportionate number of illegitimate rattlesnake envenomations (that is, those that occur when a person voluntarily approaches the snake), often to the upper extremities." In other words, young drunk men who pick up what they think are dead rattlesnakes usually get bitten.

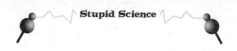

Nanu-Nanu

A group of scientists at New Mexico's Los Alamos National Laboratory believe that the future of launching satellites into space won't be with rockets but rather with an elevator. An October 14, 2003, Associated Press article disclosed that the scientists are studying, on their own time, the feasibility of building a cable shaft approximately 50,000 miles long that could be lowered to Earth from a space station, hooked to a land station, and used like an elevator to hoist supplies and even satellites. The shaft would theoretically be constructed from "carbon nanotubes" (their bonding structure is stronger than diamonds), but to date scientists can create nanotubes only a few feet long.

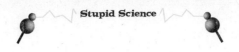
Dead Poets Society

Psychologists studied the word usage in poems by poets who later committed suicide and compared them with a control group. "One of the most telling words of all is the word 'I,'" said University of Texas researcher James Pennebaker. "People who are suicidal or depressed use 'I' at much, much higher rates, and there's also a corresponding drop in references to other people." However, Pennebaker remarked in the July 27, 2001, article in the *Telegraph*, "We're not saying that if you use 'I' a lot, then you'll commit suicide. It's just simply a marker of greater risk."

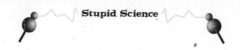

Watch Where You're Going

By studying how locusts avoid midair collisions with other locusts in a swarm, researchers at England's Newcastle University began developing an automobile collision avoidance system that uses the bugs' natural ability. Locusts have a highly developed portion of their brain called the giant lobular movement detector (GLMD), which is like crash-warning radar. In order to study the bugs, according to a July 29, 2001, article in the *Guardian*, neurobiologist Dr. Claire Rind said, "Essentially, we made little armchairs for them, and stuck them in front of TV screens," and in order to monitor the insects' GLMD reactions, they subjected the bugs to dogfight scenes from *Star Wars*.

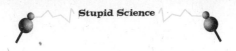

Coming and Going

Researchers at the University of Sheffield (England) conducted research into the sex life of the mealworm beetle and discovered that "organisms that mate the most, and are therefore more successful in evolutionary terms, reduce their own life expectancy in the process," said Dr. Michael Siva-Jothy. Siva-Jothy claims that a hormone is released during mating that damages the organism's immune system. A July 4, 2002, report from BBC News stated that although the research dealt with mealworms, the study's findings could also hold true for humans.

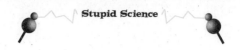

Paying a Duty on Doodie

A scientist returning from Antarctica was stopped at Florida's Miami International Airport when something in his backpack set off the airport's bomb detectors. According to a June 6, 2003, article in the *Scotsman*, a thorough search of the backpack revealed that the scientist had been carrying samples of penguin droppings, which have a high nitrate content, and because nitrates are used to produce bombs, the airport's warning device was triggered.

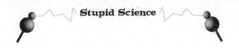

The Man Radiated Confidence

He was considered by many to be the most radioactive man on the planet. Nuclear physicist Dr. Eric Voice was eighty years old when he died on September 11, 2004, and he was an avid supporter of nuclear power who dismissed fears about the health risks of plutonium as media hype. Voice volunteered to be a human guinea pig in 1992, and he was given a series of plutonium injections and deliberately inhaled plutonium isotopes found near nuclear reactors. According to an article about his death in an October 19, 2004, article in the *Independent*, because of the radioactivity in his body, Voice's remains could not be cremated. Instead he was buried in a lead-lined coffin.

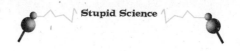
But Don't Talk with Your Mouth Full

A Cambridge University professor who conducted laboratory experiments involving kinetic energy, centrifugal force, and friction told the *National Post* of London in an April 16, 2001, article that the neatest way to eat spaghetti is to hold a spoon parallel to the plate and, holding a fork perpendicular to the spoon, wind the pasta around the tines, remove the fork, and then eat the spaghetti off the spoon.

Astolfo Gomes de Mello Araujo
and Jose Carlos Marcelino

won the

2008 Ig Nobel Prize
in
archaeology

for showing that armadillos can mix up
the contents of an archaeological site.

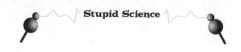

The Real Rat Pack

They're called roborats, and they're conditioned to go wherever the scientist in control wants them to go, but they're to be used primarily for rescue missions or to locate explosives. The roborats are actual lab rats that have probes inserted into their brains and connected to a radio controlled device strapped to their backs. The controller stimulates the rat's pleasure center to make it go in a desired direction. Quelling fears of mindless rodents, one researcher remarked in a May 2, 2002, Reuters article, "They're not zombies."

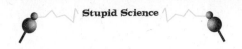

Now There Are 1,002 Uses

The Associated Press interviewed Dean Focht of the Madigan Army Medical Center in Tacoma, Washington, on October 14, 2002, about new research into the army's use of duct tape. Focht announced that the "do anything" tape can now help people remove pesky warts without freezing them off with liquid nitrogen. The suggested application is to place a piece of duct tape over the wart for about a month; this will suffocate the growth, and the remaining dead skin can be buffed away. So you won't have an unsightly wart; you'll just have a piece of unsightly silver tape for a month.

According to German researchers,
the day of the week with the
highest incidence of heart attacks is
Monday.

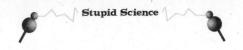

It's Her Best Feature

According to a January 15, 2004, article in the *Evening Standard*, researchers in Hong Kong claim to have determined what makes a woman attractive to a man—and no, it's not those. It's the volume–height index (VHI), which is responsible for 90 percent of a woman's initial perceived attractiveness. The researchers determined that a man makes a snap decision about a woman by looking at her overall body volume before perusing any particular feature. To determine your VHI, simply figure your volume in cubic meters and then divide the total by the square of the distance between your chin and your feet. Researchers refused to come up with the ideal VHI.

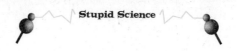

Bloated Bovine

On July 9, 2008, the *Telegraph* in London reported that scientists in Argentina had placed emission collection tanks on the backs of cows to measure the amount of methane gas the country's estimated 55 million cattle released daily. The scientists confirmed that methane retains twenty-three times more heat than carbon dioxide and is a contributing factor in global warming. Results from the Argentine National Institute of Agricultural Technology and the Argentine National Council of Scientific and Technical Investigations revealed that the average cow toots between 800 and 1,000 liters of methane daily.

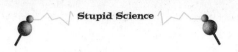

Road Trip!

Dr. Kurt Kotrschal of the Zoology Department at Austria's Vienna University admitted that a flock of domestically bred northern bald ibis refused to fly south for the winter and had to be given a lift. The *Telegraph* reported on August 27, 2003, about the flock of lazy and disoriented birds. Ornithologists from the Konrad Lorenz research center in Grünau, Austria, decided to load the birds onto trucks and drive them 500 miles to their winter retreat in northern Italy.

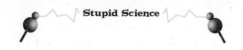

Our Six-Legged Friends

Research conducted on cockroaches at Case Western
Reserve University and reported in a January 14, 2004,
article on their Web site showed that the insects don't age
very gracefully. It was noted that after about sixty weeks of
adulthood, cockroaches suffered from both a "tarus catch," in
which the joint between its paw and front leg joint hardens,
causing the leg to bend to almost 45 degrees, and hardened
foot pads that limit the ability to climb on vertical surfaces.
Researcher Paul Schaefer showed that older cockroaches lost
their ability to elude predators, and he hypothesized that the
cause was a deficiency in the brain. He tested his hypothesis
by removing the roach's head, and therefore its brain, and the
roach scampered away as it did in its youth.

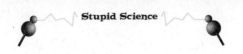

Pull My Fin

Ben Wilson, Bob Batty, and Lawrence Dill's article in the journal *Proceedings of the Royal Society* (November 2003) reported that herring communicate with each other by producing fart-like sounds. "We heard these rasping noises," said Batty, "which sound like high pitched raspberries, only at night, whenever we saw tiny gas bubbles coming from the herrings' bottoms." Which reminds me never to order herring in raspberry sauce again.

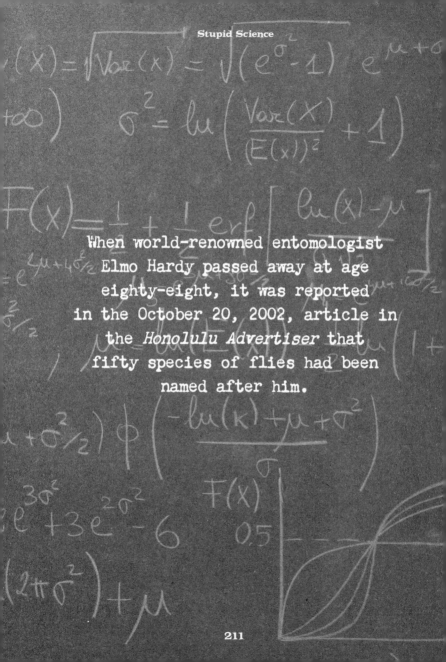

When world-renowned entomologist Elmo Hardy passed away at age eighty-eight, it was reported in the October 20, 2002, article in the *Honolulu Advertiser* that fifty species of flies had been named after him.

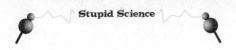
The Cat's Meow

Researchers conducted an experiment at the Dallas Zoo to see how certain species in the cat family react to various odors. The *Dallas Morning News* reported on February 28, 2000, that the zoo's four female ocelots responded most erotically to the Calvin Klein perfume called Obsession.

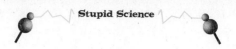

Hooked on Sex

An animal that reproduces in a most interesting way is the deep sea angler fish, according to research by scientists from Australia and New Zealand. Dr. Mark Norman, curator at Museum Victoria in Australia, illuminated the bizarre mating habits of this fish, which lives in total darkness: "The female is the size of a tennis ball. It has big savage teeth [and] a rod lure off the top of its head with a glowing tip to coax in stupid prey." The male "looks like a black jellybean with fins." According to a March 23, 2004, article in the *Independent*, the tiny male bites into the female's side, drinks her blood, and then inseminates her. Eventually, said Norman, their flesh permanently fuses together, and "they have found females with up to six males attached."

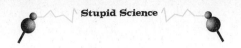

A Fly-by-Night Study

An article in the July 27, 2004, issue of *Current Biology* titled "Pigeon Homing Along Highways and Exits" summarized the results of a ten-year study with pigeons and global positioning satellites. Researchers at England's Oxford University concluded that, contrary to previously held beliefs, homing pigeons do not navigate by using the sun; rather, they simply follow roads and highways home.

IT'S A LIVING

Popular Science's "10 Worst Jobs in Science" for 2007 included the following:

- The team at Ward's Natural Science in Rochester, New York, who prepare the carcasses of cats, frogs, sharks, and even cockroaches and ship them to science classes.

- Elephant vasectomist Mark Stetter, who invented and uses a 4-foot-long fiber-optic laparoscope attached to a video monitor to sterilize the elephant's 12-inch-wide testicles.

"Scientists Isolate Animal Fart Gene"

Southland Times (Invercargill, New Zealand) headline, June 6, 2008

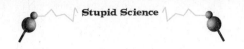

The Mouse That Roared

The "Preble's meadow jumping mouse" was placed on the endangered species list in 1998, and the rules for its protection cost landowners and governments in its habitat on the Front Range Urban Corridor of the Rockies (Colorado and Wyoming) approximately $100 million. The Endangered Species Act prohibited certain rodent control, land maintenance, and weed control practices and even ruled that, in certain areas, house cats going outdoors must be kept on a leash. But in 2005, the Denver Museum of Nature and Science found that the mouse never existed; it was identical to the Bear Lodge meadow jumping mouse, which isn't endangered. The pesky but plentiful rodent was removed from the endangered species list on July 10, 2008.

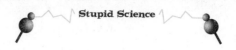
Look Who's Coming to Dinner

Beauty is in the eye of the beholder, and entomologist David George Gordon is more than just a fan of cockroaches, touting their qualities as "intelligent, hardworking and fastidious groomers." According to a March 1999 article in California's *Santa Cruz Sentinel*, Gordon praised the insects and stated that their presence is essential, especially in tropical regions, for eliminating dead animal matter. But cockroaches aren't the only bugs Gordon likes. In fact, he authored a book of bug recipes called *Eat-a-Bug Cookbook: 33 Ways to Cook Grasshoppers, Ants, Water Bugs, Spiders, Centipedes, and Their Kin*.

Take a Look at This Book

The Guinness Book of Records states that the book *Bhutan: A Visual Odyssey Across the Himalayan Kingdom*, at 133 pounds and 5 feet, 7 inches long, is the biggest book ever made. Scientist Michael Hawley of the Massachusetts Institute of Technology authored the book, whose 114 pages open to nearly 7 feet wide. According to a December 15, 2003, article in the *New York Times*, each book uses nearly a gallon of ink and enough paper to cover a football field. Hawley charges $10,000 for each printing of the book and donates the money to his charity, Friendly Planet, which builds schools in South Asia.

"Science Confirms:
Politicians Lie"

Reuters headline, May 19, 2003